# A SUPERGUIDE TO
# AQUARIUM FISH

## DICK MILLS

GALLERY BOOKS
An Imprint of W. H. Smith Publishers Inc.
112 Madison Avenue
New York City 10016

# CONTENTS

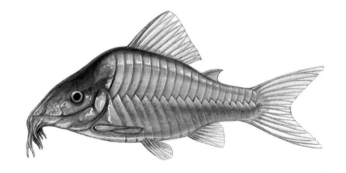

# INTRODUCTION

Some years ago, the answer to the question 'What are aquarium fishes?' would have been one word: Goldfish. That single fish, *Carassius auratus*, paved the way for today's hobby, which now embraces fishes from all over the world. Coldwater and tropical species make up the majority of fishes kept in the aquarium and garden pools, but there is a growing number of aquarists keeping tropical marine fishes from the coral reefs of the Indo-Pacific Oceans.

## FRESHWATER OR MARINE?

The most popular aquarium fishes are tropical freshwater species. The colours of the numerous species are more varied than those of their coldwater counterparts and more can be kept in a standard tank than coldwater species. Many freshwater species, whether tropical or coldwater, will breed in the aquarium. Most may be kept in water from the domestic supply, even though its hardness may vary from one part of the country to another.

Marine fishkeeping is a relatively young branch of the hobby and is more problematic for novice fishkeepers. Unlike freshwater species, marine fishes require the addition of salt to the aquarium water. Usually synthetic seawater is used, made from proprietary brands of aquarium seawater salt mixes, although salt water may be collected (from an unpolluted source) by aquarists living near the sea. Instead of decorating marine aquariums with plants, which would be unable to survive in the salt water, a variety of decorative corals can be used.

The attraction of the brilliantly coloured, tropical marine fishes is obvious but they tend to be more expensive than tropical freshwater species. Coldwater marine fishes are cheaper but the choice of species is much more limited and the fishes are generally plainer.

## PHYSICAL CHARACTERISTICS

Although fishes, whether freshwater or marine, show a variety of different shapes in adulthood, they share certain basic physical characteristics. These may be modified to suit the fish's environment.

The *fins* may be paired, or single, and are used for locomotion and stability. The small, non-functioning *adipose fin* is not always present. The anal fin of male livebearing fishes is modified into a *gonopodium*, the reproductive organ. The *mouth* is situated to suit the fish's feeding habits

Vallisneria

Cryptocoryne

Aponogeton

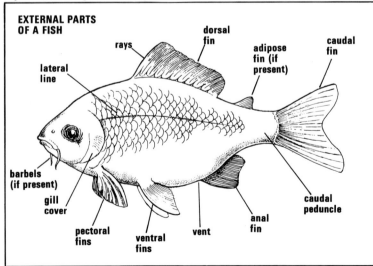

**EXTERNAL PARTS OF A FISH**

rays
dorsal fin
adipose fin (if present)
caudal fin
lateral line
barbels (if present)
gill cover
pectoral fins
ventral fins
vent
anal fin
caudal peduncle

Echinodorus
(Amazon Sword Plant)

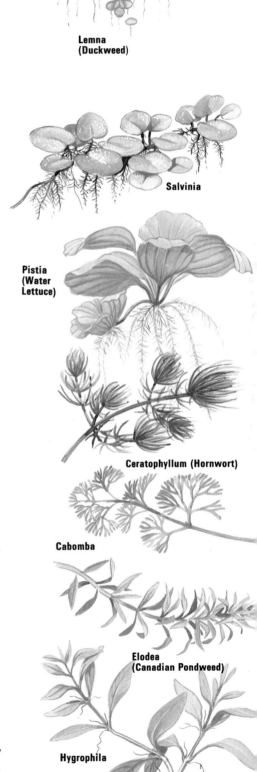

Lemna
(Duckweed)

Salvinia

Pistia
(Water
Lettuce)

Ceratophyllum (Hornwort)

Cabomba

Elodea
(Canadian Pondweed)

Hygrophila

– upturned for surface feeders, underslung for bottom and algae feeders. The *barbels* are taste-sensitive, whisker-like growths around the mouths of some fishes, and are particularly highly developed in bottom-dwelling fishes such as Catfishes (pages 18–19). The *gills* are the fish's respiratory organs, extracting dissolved oxygen from the water, although some fishes have auxiliary organs which allow them to breathe atmospheric air if necessary. The *lateral line* is a sensory system; vibrations in the water are detected through a row of openings along the flanks of the fish which are connected to nerve endings.

## FISH CLASSIFICATION AND SIZES

All fishes are classified scientifically by a *binomial system*, a generic name followed by a specific name; thus, *Barbus oligolepis* and *Barbus titteya* are two species within the genus *Barbus*, but *Moenkhausia oligolepis* is a totally unrelated fish within the genus *Moenkhausia*, although it bears a similar specific name.

Freshwater fish sizes quoted here are those expected to be attained in aquarium-kept fishes, not necessarily those of adult fishes in the wild. Sizes for marine fishes are based upon natural proportions, but these may not necessarily be attained by fishes in captivity. The fishes illustrated are adult males, unless stated otherwise.

## AQUARIUM PLANTS

Apart from their visual beauty, aquatic plants play a very important part in the natural cycle of the aquarium, helping to purify the water, absorbing carbon dioxide during photosynthesis (during the aquarium's illuminated period), providing spawning sites, and offering refuges for the young fishes. The many species of plants suitable for the aquarium may be divided into three groups.

## ROOTED PLANTS

Species in this group include the grass-like *Vallisneria* and *Sagittaria*, ideal for masking the glass walls of the tank. Species of *Cryptocoryne* provide broader-leaved plants to carpet the bottom of the tank, whilst *Aponogeton* and *Echinodorus* genera include taller-growing species to act as specimen plants, focal points in the aquarium's furnishings. Most rooted plants propagate by sending out runners from which young plants develop and which may be separated from the parent plant and re-rooted elsewhere. *Aponogeton* species, which have tuberous rhizomes rather than roots, flower above the water surface, and seeds may be obtained from the pollinated flowers.

## CUTTINGS

Although not a natural plant group, the plants in this group grow rapidly and cuttings may be taken regularly for re-rooting. Typical species are *Cabomba, Ceratophyllum, Myriophyllum, Elodea, Hygrophila* and *Limnophila*. These species of plants are often used as spawning media by the egg-scattering fishes, but may be browsed upon by fishes preferring some vegetable matter in their diet.

## FLOATING PLANTS

A number of plant species float on the water surface, their trailing roots giving refuge for the fry of breeding fishes; some Anabantid fishes use fragments of these plants in the construction of their bubblenests. *Lemna, Riccia* and *Salvinia* are all suitable for the aquarium although their rapid growth is often annoying; netfuls may be removed and fed to plant-eating fishes. *Pistia*, the Water Lettuce, often outgrows the tank.

5

# CYPRINIDS

With their bright colours, hearty appetites and constant activity it is not hard to understand the popularity of this group of fishes with the aquarist. This family has 1500 species, both tropical and coldwater. India and the Far East are the natural homes of the Barbs, Rasboras and Danios, whilst the Goldfish and Koi, originally cultured in China and Japan, now occupy many ornamental lakes in other countries.

Cyprinid fishes have no teeth in the jaws, but rely on pharyngeal teeth in the throat to break up their food. Many of the species have barbels – taste-sensitive, whisker-like growths around the mouth – which they use when rummaging around the tank gravel for food.

Cyprinids are sociable, even gregarious, and feel happier (and look better too) in shoals. Barbs are Bream-like fishes native to Africa and Asia that tend to swim in the lower levels of the aquarium. Some Barbs tend to be boisterous, and a solitary specimen amongst other fishes may develop into a fin-nipper – perhaps out of sheer boredom. Rasboras are slender fishes that usually swim in large schools in the upper levels of tropical waters. Danios are hardy and undemanding shoaling fishes similar in habits to the Rasboras. They will swim in both upper and middle levels in a tank.

**Cyprinidae
(distribution in blue)**

## FAMILY CYPRINIDAE

**Arulius Barb**

## BARBS

**Arulius Barb, Longfin Barb** *Barbus aurulius* 105 mm 4 in. South-east India: still and running water. The scarlet tips to the caudal fin and the blue-green sheen to the scales above the lateral line make for a colourful fish. Two half-completed dark transverse bands with intermediate blotches adorn the flanks, and the belly may take on a pinkish hue. The chief feature is the extension of the dorsal fin into long filaments in mature males. *Temperature:* 24°C (75°F). *Diet:* live and dry foods accepted. *Breeding:* not prolific. A notorious egg-eater.

**Rosy Barb** *Barbus conchonius* 100 mm 4 in. Northern India, Assam, Bengal: still and running water. This well-established aquarium favourite grows larger in nature, and specimens over 125 mm (5 in) have been reported. The male's colour changes from dark bronze/green to an intense rosy-red during breeding. The fins are

black. A long-finned strain has recently been introduced to the hobby, but it is a man-made variety, not a natural occurrence. *Temperature:* 24°C (75°F). *Diet:* will eat anything. *Breeding:* very prolific.

**Striped Barb; Zebra Barb** *Barbus fasciatus* 100 mm 4 in. Malaysia: all kinds of water. A proportionately longer fish with dark horizontal lines on a golden yellow body. These lines may be incomplete in young specimens, only developing into continuous lines with maturity. Some confusion may occur between this fish and *B. lineatus*, which is almost identical. However, *B. lineatus* has no barbels. An active fish, constantly patrolling its tank, which should be large enough to accommodate several specimens. *Temperature:* 24°C (75°F) *Diet:* live and dried foods. *Breeding* none reported as yet.

**Tiger Barb; Sumatra Barb** *Barbus tetrazona* 57 mm 2¼ in. Sumatra: all waters. Perhaps the most popular Barb with hobbyists. Four dark, vertical bands cross its bronze/tan body, but the fish is made additionally attractive by the black, red-edged dorsal and anal fins of the males, which may also have red snouts. Females are less brightly coloured but may have red, paired fins. This fish has been bred into several colour varieties, such as Albino, Green and Blue. Often guilty of fin-nipping and particularly of persecuting slower-moving, longer-finned fishes. A cure may be to add more Tiger Barbs to provide company or competition. *Temperature:* 24°C (75°F). *Diet:* all foods. *Breeding:* not difficult.

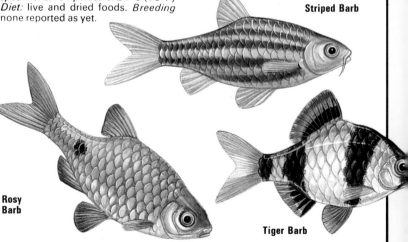

**Striped Barb**

**Rosy Barb**

**Tiger Barb**

**Golden Dwarf Barb** *Barbus gelius* 38 mm 1½ in. Central India: slow-moving, densely vegetated waters. The smallest of the Barb family, this species appears to have gone out of favour with aquarists recently, possibly because it is not so highly coloured as its relatives. The body is suffused with a golden sheen, and there are dark patches on the flanks. The male fishes may have a reddish band running from head to tail following the lateral line. Fins may be yellowish. *Temperature:* 20°C (68°F); may be reduced a little during winter. *Diet:* all small foods, both live and dried. *Breeding:* possible, fry very small. Breeding temperature not to exceed 22°C (72°F).

**Black Ruby Barb; Purple-headed Barb** *Barbus nigrofasciatus* 65 mm 2½ in. Sri Lanka: slow-moving water. Another fish in which the male's coloration is transformed at breeding time. Normally a dull yellow-gold body with three or four dark, transverse bands and sooty-coloured fins; when in prime condition, the male turns a deep, rich ruby colour and the fins darken to jet black. The scales take on an iridescence and can show a green tinge in reflected light. Females are less colourful and do not change at breeding time. *Temperature:* 24°C (75°F). *Diet:* all foods. *Breeding:* prolific; temperature may be raised a little to induce spawning.

**Checker Barb; Island Barb** *Barbus oligolepis* 50 mm 2 in. Indonesia, Sumatra: all waters. This fish may be recognized instantly by its dark-edged scales, which give it a checkered appearance. A metallic, purple sheen is more obvious in the male's colouring above the lateral line, and the dorsal and anal fins of the male fish are dark-edged. The female is less colourful and tends towards a dull yellowish brown. *Temperature:* 24°C (75°F). *Diet:* all foods. *Breeding:* ready breeders.

**Golden Barb** *Barbus schuberti* 70 mm 2¾ in. The origins of this fish are obscure; it appears to be a man-made variety, probably from *Barbus semifasciolatus* stock (a very similar fish but of greenish-yellow hue), but another ancestor may be *Barbus*

*sachsi.* A bright yellow fish with red fins, the males having more dark flecks on the flanks than the females, which, in their turn, may be more recognizable by their plumpness when viewed from above. Sometimes this fish suffers from 'blood-blisters' on the body and in the fins. *Temperature:* 24°C (75°F). *Diet:* all foods. *Breeding:* prolific.

**Tinfoil Barb; Goldfoil Barb; Schwanenfeld's Barb** *Barbus schwanenfeldi* 300 mm 12 in. The largest Barb. The scales reflect like bright tin, with the scales near the dorsal surface having a golden sheen. The fins are bright red, with the caudal and dorsal being edged with black. This active fish will spend the day cruising up and down the tank eating anything that comes its way — including plants. It does not attack other fishes but may cause them some discomfort by its sheer size and turbulence as it passes. Obviously needs a large tank and may become the favourite of its owner. Plastic plants may be used to decorate the aquarium if necessary, but must be anchored down securely. Young fishes are very attractive, and are often purchased in ignorance of their likely adult size by newcomers to the hobby. *Temperature:* 24°C (75°F). *Diet:* all foods, see above. *Breeding:* has been bred in large aquaria.

**Cherry Barb** *Barbus titteya* 50 mm 2 in. Sri Lanka: densely planted waters. Similar in size, but more elongate than the Checker Barb, the Cherry Barb has an even, speckled patterning which is more intense above the lateral line. A dark band runs from snout to caudal fin in both sexes, with a faint gold line above it. Males may have a metallic sheen to the area above the line and their predominant coloration is cherry red; females are more of a drab red-brown. The male's colours are intensified when in the presence of a ripe female, and the male often stretches and displays his fins so energetically that they may split. This species may be a little shy, and thickets of refuge-giving plants are welcomed. *Temperature:* 24°C (75°F). *Diet:* all foods, including vegetable matter such as soft algae scrapings from the tank glass. *Breeding:* usual Barb methods.

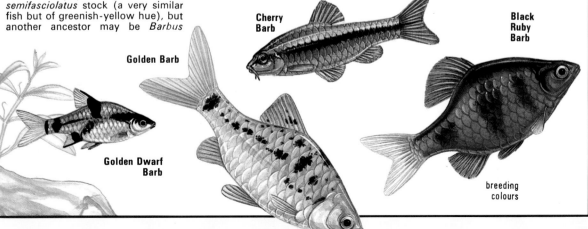

Checker Barb

Tinfoil Barb

Golden Barb

Cherry Barb

Golden Dwarf Barb

Black Ruby Barb

breeding colours

# RASBORAS

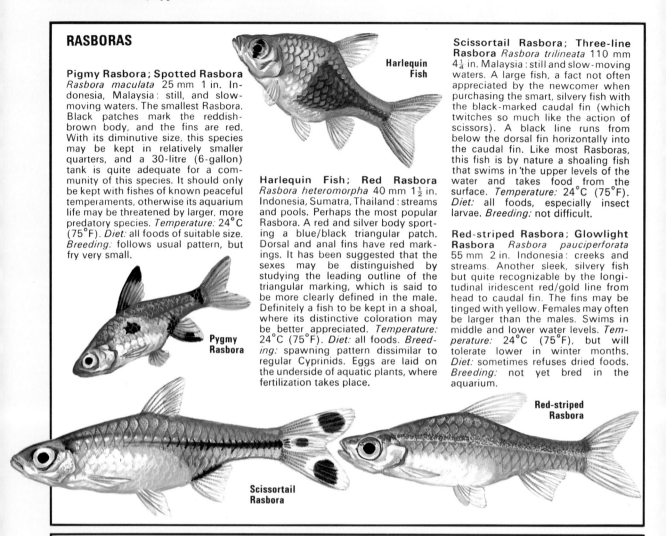

Harlequin
Fish

**Pigmy Rasbora; Spotted Rasbora**
*Rasbora maculata* 25 mm 1 in. Indonesia, Malaysia: still, and slow-moving waters. The smallest Rasbora. Black patches mark the reddish-brown body, and the fins are red. With its diminutive size, this species may be kept in relatively smaller quarters, and a 30-litre (6-gallon) tank is quite adequate for a community of this species. It should only be kept with fishes of known peaceful temperaments, otherwise its aquarium life may be threatened by larger, more predatory species. *Temperature:* 24°C (75°F). *Diet:* all foods of suitable size. *Breeding:* follows usual pattern, but fry very small.

**Harlequin Fish; Red Rasbora**
*Rasbora heteromorpha* 40 mm 1½ in. Indonesia, Sumatra, Thailand: streams and pools. Perhaps the most popular Rasbora. A red and silver body sporting a blue/black triangular patch. Dorsal and anal fins have red markings. It has been suggested that the sexes may be distinguished by studying the leading outline of the triangular marking, which is said to be more clearly defined in the male. Definitely a fish to be kept in a shoal, where its distinctive coloration may be better appreciated. *Temperature:* 24°C (75°F). *Diet:* all foods. *Breeding:* spawning pattern dissimilar to regular Cyprinids. Eggs are laid on the underside of aquatic plants, where fertilization takes place.

**Scissortail Rasbora; Three-line Rasbora** *Rasbora trilineata* 110 mm 4¼ in. Malaysia: still and slow-moving waters. A large fish, a fact not often appreciated by the newcomer when purchasing the smart, silvery fish with the black-marked caudal fin (which twitches so much like the action of scissors). A black line runs from below the dorsal fin horizontally into the caudal fin. Like most Rasboras, this fish is by nature a shoaling fish that swims in 'the upper levels of the water and takes food from the surface. *Temperature:* 24°C (75°F). *Diet:* all foods, especially insect larvae. *Breeding:* not difficult.

**Red-striped Rasbora; Glowlight Rasbora** *Rasbora pauciperforata* 55 mm 2 in. Indonesia: creeks and streams. Another sleek, silvery fish but quite recognizable by the longitudinal iridescent red/gold line from head to caudal fin. The fins may be tinged with yellow. Females may often be larger than the males. Swims in middle and lower water levels. *Temperature:* 24°C (75°F), but will tolerate lower in winter months. *Diet:* sometimes refuses dried foods. *Breeding:* not yet bred in the aquarium.

Pygmy
Rasbora

Red-striped
Rasbora

Scissortail
Rasbora

# DANIOS

**Pearl Danio** *Brachydanio albolineatus* 57 mm 2¼ in. South-east Asia: paddy fields, still and slow-moving waters. An active, medium-sized fish with a blue, pearl lustre to its flanks. A gold horizontal line extends rearwards from below the dorsal fin into the caudal fin and is bordered by blue/violet bands. The fins are yellowish. The beauty of this fish is appreciated better when viewed in reflected light. Females may be recognized by the well-tried method of viewing from above, when their plumpness is easily seen. This fish needs plenty of swimming space. There is a gold variant called the Golden Danio. *Temperature:* 24°C (75°F). *Diet:* all foods. *Breeding:* a ready spawner.

**Leopard Danio** *Brachydanio frankei* 57 mm 2¼ in. A popular fish, easily recognized by the similarity in markings to its namesake in the mammal kingdom. It may not occur in nature but may have originated in the aquarium as a *sport* (a freak, patterned fish in an otherwise normal spawning of, perhaps, *Brachydanio rerio* or *Brachydanio nigrofasciatus*). Females are noticeably fuller in body depth when ripe. *Temperature:* 24°C (75°F). *Diet:* all foods. *Breeding:* straightforward.

**Zebra Danio; Zebra Fish** *Brachydanio rerio* 50 mm 2 in. Eastern India: paddy fields and slow-moving waters. The most popular and best-known of all the Danios. Its common name describes it precisely: horizontal stripes of royal blue (appearing darker because of their narrowness) cover the silver/gold body from head to tail. The stripes are continued into the fins of the male, but only to a lesser extent in the female. An active fish, and once again a shoal is to be recommended. *Temperature:* 24°C (75°F). *Diet:* all foods. *Breeding:* easy; may be spawned as a shoal.

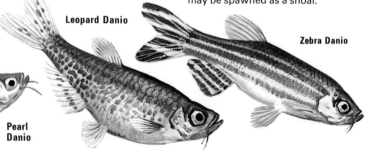

Leopard Danio

Zebra Danio

Pearl
Danio

# OTHER TROPICAL CYPRINIDS

Flying Fox

Red-tailed
Black Shark

Silver
Shark

White Cloud
Mountain Minnow

Garnet
Minnow

**Flying Fox** *Epalzeorhynchus kallopterus* 140 mm 5½ in. Borneo, Indonesia, Java, Sumatra: densely vegetated creeks. A long, torpedo-shaped fish, with the belly flattened and the mouth underslung. A wide, dark band topped with bright yellow runs horizontally from the snout into the caudal fin. The reddish fins are marked with black areas and tipped with white. Often perches on rocks or broad-leafed plants when at rest. Sometimes takes exception to other members of its own species. *Temperature:* 24°C (75°F). *Diet:* the fringed lips indicate an algae-eating browser, but live and dried foods taken. *Breeding:* not yet bred in the aquarium.

**Silver Shark; Bala Shark; Tricolor Shark** *Balantiocheilus melanopterus* 350 mm 13¾ in. Borneo, Sumatra, Thailand: running waters. Although misnamed, a very smart fish. An elongated fish of bluish-silver coloration in general. The main attraction lies in the fins; these are yellow, edged with thick black margins, while the caudal fin also has a red area between the yellow and black. A very fast swimmer, and will also jump. Impressive in shoals. *Temperature:* 24°C (75°F). *Diet:* all foods. *Breeding:* no information available.

**Red-tailed Black Shark** *Labeo bicolor* 150 mm 6 in. Thailand: various waters. The large dorsal fin and underslung mouth are responsible for the reference to the shark in the common name, but this fish is not related to the saltwater species in any way. The rest of the common name, however, describes the fish exactly — everything is black except for the bright, orange-red caudal fin. Can be territorially minded and often attacks intruders. *Temperature:* 25°C (77°F). *Diet:* should include vegetable matter. Often browses on algae and soft-leaved plants. *Breeding:* difficult in the aquarium.

**Garnet Minnow** *Hemigrammocypris lini* 50 mm 2 in. China: probably running waters. A recent addition to the hobby and, at first sight, may be attributed to the Rasbora group. A silver-bronze fish with a dark line running horizontally from head to caudal fin bordered above by gold. There is a small dark spot at the base of the caudal fin. Very active in the aquarium. *Temperature:* 24°C (75°F), perhaps slightly lower. *Diet:* all foods. *Breeding:* although a 'new' fish, it has proved to be a ready spawner.

**White Cloud Mountain Minnow; Tan's Fish** *Tanichthys albonubes* 45 mm 1¾ in. China: probably running water. A borderline 'tropical', as it thrives quite happily at lower than 'normal' tropical temperatures. A feature of this fish is its iridescent blue-green horizontal line, from eye to caudal fin. The body colour is dark olive-brown. The fins are yellow, tipped with red. There is still some confusion between this fish and another almost identical species, *Aphyocypris pooni;* colour differences are said to occur in the fins (which have a red base and yellow margin tipped with blue in *A. pooni*), but some sources suggest that the two fishes are only sub-species of the same genus. *Temperature:* 16-24°C (61-75°F). *Diet:* all foods. *Breeding:* not difficult; may be spawned in outside ponds in summer as a shoal. Fry generally ignored by the parents.

# COLDWATER CYPRINIDS

Bitterling

female spawning

Bristol Shubunkin

Common Goldfish

Comet

Celestial

Fantail

Veiltail

**Bitterling** *Rhodeus amarus* 80 mm 3¼ in. Europe: various waters. Has a violet, blue-green iridescent sheen to the body. A horizontal blue-green line extends rearwards from below the large dorsal fin to the caudal fin, where it terminates in a red spot. The fins and the eyes may also be reddish. Although it may rival its tropical relations in its colouring, the Bitterling's main attraction to the aquarist is its method of reproduction. Eggs are laid, via a long, extended ovipositor, into the inlet siphon of a freshwater bivalve, the Painter's Mussel or the Swan Mussel. The male Bitterling's fertilizing milt is drawn into the Mussel during its respiratory cycle and fertilization of the eggs occurs. The fry then develop inside the Mussel. The secret of spawning Bitterlings successfully lies in the aquarist's ability to maintain the host Mussel in the aquarium, as the fishes themselves present no problems. *Temperature:* 4-22°C (39-72°F). *Diet:* all foods. *Breeding:* see above.

**Goldfish** *Carassius auratus* Although an aquarium favourite for many years, the common Goldfish is perhaps more suitable for pond life, where it can even survive beneath ice. However, genetic experimentation by aquarists has produced many fascinating Fancy Goldfish varieties that do better in the confines of the aquarium, being too delicate to withstand the rigours of the outdoor pond. Of these varieties, the beginner should gain experience with the singletail species before graduating to the more demanding twintails. Due to their foraging habits when searching for food, the Fancy Goldfish's tank should be furnished with well-rooted plants that are perhaps protected with small pebbles around the crown to prevent uprooting. Undergravel filtration is not suitable for such an aquarium and external or box filters may do a better job of maintaining water clarity. Goldfish are not difficult to feed; in the pond they will eat insects and worms that fall into the pool, whilst in the indoor aquarium live and dried foods, even household scraps, are readily accepted. But, particularly in the case of the more exotic forms, the tank must be kept clean at all times and uneaten food and detritus regularly removed.

# LOACHES

The anatomy of the Loaches reflects the fact that the fishes are bottom-dwelling – their undersides are flat and they have underslung mouths, complete with barbels (page 6). In the aquarium, Loaches may be nocturnal, although some soon lose their shyness and venture around the tank during its illuminated periods. The fishes often make hiding places by burrowing under rocks or into a tangle of aquarium plants. Most prefer to live in a community rather than as solitary specimens. The majority of Loaches have erectile spines which may catch in the aquarist's net.

Cobitidae

## FAMILY COBITIDAE

**Kuhli Loach; Coolie Loach** *Acanthophthalmus kuhli* 110 mm 4½ in. South-east Asia : streams and rivers. This genus gets its name, meaning 'thorn-eye', from the spine over the eye. It has a worm-like body, flattened laterally at the caudal peduncle, and an underslung mouth with barbels. A pink/yellow coloration, with two or three dark bands encircling the head and gill cover. A large number of dark bands (often split longitudinally) almost ring the rest of the body, but do not cover the belly. The fins are colourless. Frequents tangles of plant roots and may form a tangled mass with its brothers and sisters. Several species of *Acanthophthalmus* are available. *Temperature:* 24°C (75°F). *Diet:* worms, but will scavenge for other foods. *Breeding:* possible.

**Skunk Botia; Hora's Loach; Mouse Loach** *Botia horae* 90 mm 3½ in. Indonesia : slow-moving waters. An attractive smaller Loach in this group. A grey/green body with a dark line running from the snout along the top of the back and crossing the body immediately in front of the caudal fin. The scales are very small, and fishes of this genus appear to have a matt finish. Some may have thin transverse lines on the flanks. The erectile spine is carried below the eye. A fairly active fish, but it may be timid if alone in a community collection. *Temperature:* 24°C (75°F). *Diet:* prefers worms and insect larvae, but will take dried foods, often in mid-water. *Breeding:* no information available.

**Clown Loach; Tiger Botia** *Botia macracantha* 200 mm 8 in. Indonesia : slow-moving waters. A very attractive fish. Three black bands encircle the bright orange body. The dorsal and anal fins are black with orange edges ; the other fins are red, with streaks of black in the caudal fin. Susceptible to White Spot disease, and some sources suggest that medicants are not well tolerated. This species grows much larger in nature. *Temperature:* 24°C (75°F). *Diet:* as for *B. horae*. *Breeding:* not yet bred in the aquarium regularly, but spawning has been reported.

**Zebra Loach** *Botia striata* 85 mm 3½ in. India : slow-moving waters. The body is covered in a large number of narrow, dark stripes. The snout is not so pointed as in other species. The fins are patterned. A slow-growing species. Fairly shy, often given up for dead due to its non-appearance, but a hardy fish. *Temperature:* 24°C (75°F). *Diet:* as for *B. horae*. *Breeding:* not yet bred in the aquarium.

**Chain Loach; Dwarf Loach** *Botia sidthimunki* 55 mm 2¼ in. Far East: slow-moving waters. The smallest of the Botias, this species has a gold body marked with a dark, chain-link pattern down to midway across the flanks. The lower links may join to form a horizontal line. The fins are clear, except for the caudal fin, which bears some patterning. Less timid than other Loaches, it enjoys the company of its own species. *Temperature:* 24°C (75°F). *Diet:* all foods. *Breeding:* not yet bred in the aquarium.

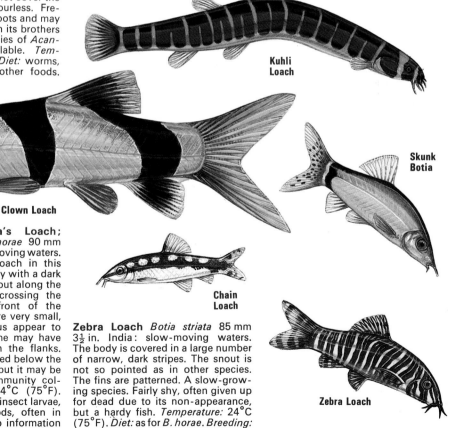

Kuhli Loach

Skunk Botia

Clown Loach

Chain Loach

Zebra Loach

# CHARACINS

This large group of fishes contains over 1300 species, some of which are suitable for the aquarium. Most come from Central and South America, although there are a few species from Africa and North America. A family characteristic is the possession of an adipose fin (page 4), although some species are without it. Unlike other fins, the adipose does not help the fish to swim or balance. All Characins have teeth, and most are of carnivorous appetite. These brightly coloured fishes are always happier in a shoal and may be induced to spawn in captivity without too much trouble. Although preferring soft, acid water, the fishes are hardy enough to adapt to most domestic water supplies.

Characidae

## FAMILY CHARACIDAE

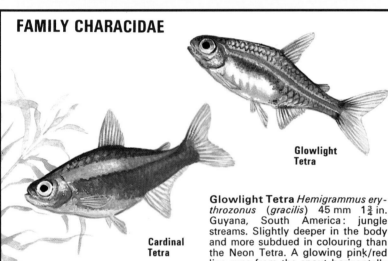

Glowlight Tetra

Cardinal Tetra

**Cardinal Tetra** *Cheirodon axelrodi* 50 mm 2 in. South America: the Amazon and jungle streams. A truly gorgeous fish. An electric-blue-green horizontal stripe runs from snout to adipose fin. Below it a broad band of scarlet covers the rest of the body, with the exception of a silver/white belly. The fins are colourless, except for the caudal, which has some continuation of the red of the body. *Temperature:* 24°C (75°F). *Diet:* all foods. *Breeding:* spawnings have been reported.

**Neon Tetra** *Paracheirodon innesi* 45 mm 1¾ in. South America: jungle streams. Until the introduction of the Cardinal Tetra, this was the jewel of the aquarium. Colouring is almost identical, except that the red band does not extend the whole length of the body but covers only the rear half. Females may be deeper in the body and, when full of roe, their extra plumpness may cause a visible bend in the blue-green line. *Temperature:* 24°C (75°F). *Diet:* all foods. *Breeding:* has been spawned in as little as a litre (2 pints) of water of various hardnesses.

**Glowlight Tetra** *Hemigrammus erythrozonus* (*gracilis*) 45 mm 1¾ in. Guyana, South America: jungle streams. Slightly deeper in the body and more subdued in colouring than the Neon Tetra. A glowing pink/red line runs from the snout horizontally along the body to terminate in a red area at the base of the caudal fin. The area above this line is brown, silver below. The dorsal and anal fins have a rosy patch and may be tipped with white. Females are deeper in the body. *Temperature:* 24°C (75°F). *Diet:* all foods. *Breeding:* egg scattering. Soft water for breeding is advantageous.

**Head and Tail Light Tetra; Beacon Fish** *Hemigrammus ocellifer* 45 mm 1¾ in. South America: various waters. The red/gold eye and the gold patch at the base of the caudal fin provide the common name of this fish. A dark line runs horizontally along the rear half of the body, broadening into a dark area at the base of the caudal fin. The fins may have blue/white edgings or tips. Males may have a dark shoulder patch highlighted by a gold surround. *Temperature:* 24°C (75°F). *Diet:* all foods. *Breeding:* egg scattering.

**Rummy-nosed Tetra; Red-nosed Tetra** *Hemigrammus rhodostomus* 55 mm 2¼ in. South America: jungle streams. A silvery fish whose main coloration is provided by the bright red snout and head and the black and white, horizontally striped caudal fin. A thin, dark line runs from below the dorsal fin into the middle dark stripe of the caudal fin; another dark line runs from the anal fin rearwards along the ventral contour of the body. *Temperature:* 24°C (75°F). *Diet:* all foods. *Breeding:* difficult, because this is a shy and very sensitive species.

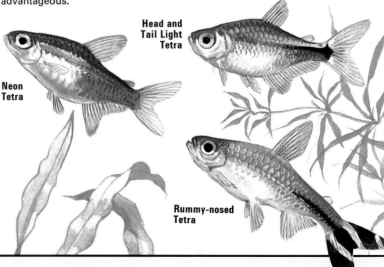

Head and Tail Light Tetra

Neon Tetra

Rummy-nosed Tetra

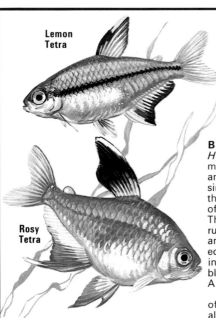

**Lemon Tetra**

**Bloodfin**

**Rosy Tetra**

**Lemon Tetra** *Hyphessobrycon pulchripinnis* 50 mm 2 in. South America: various waters. A delicate lemon-yellow body, with a red iris to the eye. An albino form exists, but only in aquaria. The leading edge of the partially black anal fin is bright yellow. The dorsal fin may have a black edge or tip. *Temperature:* 24°C (75°F). *Diet:* all foods. *Breeding:* possible.

**Rosy Tetra; Rosaceous Tetra** *Hyphessobrycon rosaceus* 50 mm 2 in. South America: various waters. Pink or rosy body colour, the fins similarly coloured, with the caudal fin having deep red in the lobes. The male's anal fin may be edged with black, and the dorsal is sickle-shaped, black, and tipped with white. Females are deeper in the body. There is some confusion between this species and *H. ornatus. Temperature:* 24°C (75°F). *Diet:* all foods. *Breeding:* possible. A slight rise in temperature may be beneficial.

**Bleeding Heart Tetra; Tetra Perez** *Hyphessobrycon erythrostigma* 70 mm 2¾ in. South America: streams and rivers. This larger Tetra has a similar body shape and colouring to the Rosy Tetra, but with the addition of a red spot just behind the gills. There may be a pink/violet band running along the lateral line. The anal fin is white, with a black and pink edging. The dorsal fin (sickle-shaped in the male) is pink/mauve with a black area, and the tip may be white. A dark vertical line crosses the eye.

A striking fish, but it seems to be of a nervous disposition, often being alarmed by the aquarist's presence near the tank. This species was formerly known as *H. rubrostigma. Temperature:* 24°C (75°F). *Diet:* all foods. *Breeding:* difficult.

**Serpae Tetra** *Hyphessobrycon serpae* 45 mm 1¾ in. South America: various waters. A fish which may be classified under several names (*H. callistus, H. bentosi, H. minor*), because the colour patterns vary with age and interbreeding of the species occurs. A blood-red body, with a black-edged anal fin, a black area over most of the dorsal fin, and a black, diamond-shaped mark on the shoulder. In some circles this fish has the reputation of being a fin-nipper of other fishes. *Temperature:* 24°C (75°F). *Diet:* all foods. *Breeding:* possible.

**X-ray Tetra; X-ray Fish; Riddle's Tetra** *Pristella maxillaris* (*riddlei*) 45 mm 1¾ in. A silvery body colour. The almost transparent body allows internal organs to be seen. The caudal fin is red, the remaining fins yellow and black, tipped with white. A horizontal dark line is sometimes prominent. *Temperature:* 24°C (75°F). *Diet:* all foods. *Breeding:* avid egg eaters, so egg-saving essential.

**Black Widow; Petticoat Fish; Blackamoor; Butterfly Tetra** *Gymnocorymbus ternetzi* 60 mm 2½ in. South America: various waters. A deep and laterally compressed body, silver in colour with the rear half black. A black vertical stripe passes through the eye. Two black, vertical bars almost cross the body between the gill cover and the dorsal fin. A long-finned variety has recently been introduced. *Temperature:* 24°C (75°F). *Diet:* all foods. *Breeding:* possible.

**Bloodfin** *Aphyocharax rubripinnis* 60 mm 2½ in. South America: various waters. The Characin equivalent of the Cyprinid shoaling fishes. Active, upper water-level swimmer. Silver body. Ventral and anal fins and lower base of the caudal fin are blood-red. Males have tiny hooks on the anal fin, which occasionally catch in the aquarist's net. An almost identical species, *A. dentatus,* has less red on the caudal fin and is known as the False Bloodfin. *Temperature:* 24°C (75°F). *Diet:* all foods. *Breeding:* egg eaters.

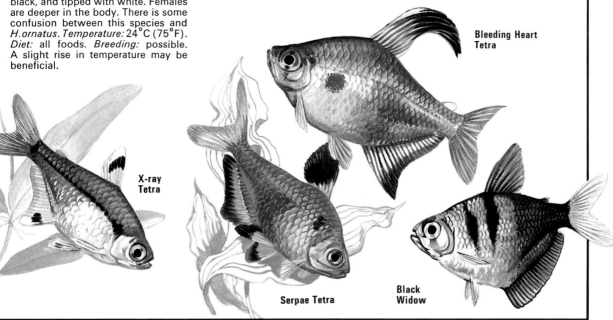

**Bleeding Heart Tetra**

**X-ray Tetra**

**Serpae Tetra**

**Black Widow**

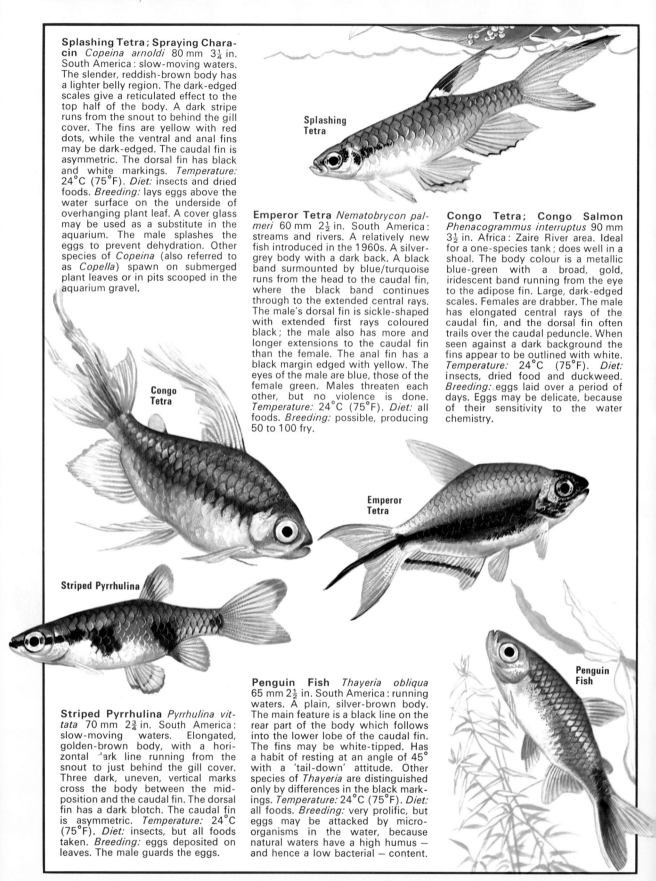

**Splashing Tetra; Spraying Characin** *Copeina arnoldi* 80 mm $3\frac{1}{4}$ in. South America : slow-moving waters. The slender, reddish-brown body has a lighter belly region. The dark-edged scales give a reticulated effect to the top half of the body. A dark stripe runs from the snout to behind the gill cover. The fins are yellow with red dots, while the ventral and anal fins may be dark-edged. The caudal fin is asymmetric. The dorsal fin has black and white markings. *Temperature:* 24°C (75°F). *Diet:* insects and dried foods. *Breeding:* lays eggs above the water surface on the underside of overhanging plant leaf. A cover glass may be used as a substitute in the aquarium. The male splashes the eggs to prevent dehydration. Other species of *Copeina* (also referred to as *Copella*) spawn on submerged plant leaves or in pits scooped in the aquarium gravel.

Splashing Tetra

Congo Tetra

Emperor Tetra

Striped Pyrrhulina

Penguin Fish

**Emperor Tetra** *Nematobrycon palmeri* 60 mm $2\frac{1}{2}$ in. South America : streams and rivers. A relatively new fish introduced in the 1960s. A silver-grey body with a dark back. A black band surmounted by blue/turquoise runs from the head to the caudal fin, where the black band continues through to the extended central rays. The male's dorsal fin is sickle-shaped with extended first rays coloured black; the male also has more and longer extensions to the caudal fin than the female. The anal fin has a black margin edged with yellow. The eyes of the male are blue, those of the female green. Males threaten each other, but no violence is done. *Temperature:* 24°C (75°F). *Diet:* all foods. *Breeding:* possible, producing 50 to 100 fry.

**Congo Tetra; Congo Salmon** *Phenacogrammus interruptus* 90 mm $3\frac{1}{2}$ in. Africa : Zaire River area. Ideal for a one-species tank ; does well in a shoal. The body colour is a metallic blue-green with a broad, gold, iridescent band running from the eye to the adipose fin. Large, dark-edged scales. Females are drabber. The male has elongated central rays of the caudal fin, and the dorsal fin often trails over the caudal peduncle. When seen against a dark background the fins appear to be outlined with white. *Temperature:* 24°C (75°F). *Diet:* insects, dried food and duckweed. *Breeding:* eggs laid over a period of days. Eggs may be delicate, because of their sensitivity to the water chemistry.

**Striped Pyrrhulina** *Pyrrhulina vittata* 70 mm $2\frac{3}{4}$ in. South America : slow-moving waters. Elongated, golden-brown body, with a horizontal dark line running from the snout to just behind the gill cover. Three dark, uneven, vertical marks cross the body between the mid-position and the caudal fin. The dorsal fin has a dark blotch. The caudal fin is asymmetric. *Temperature:* 24°C (75°F). *Diet:* insects, but all foods taken. *Breeding:* eggs deposited on leaves. The male guards the eggs.

**Penguin Fish** *Thayeria obliqua* 65 mm $2\frac{1}{2}$ in. South America : running waters. A plain, silver-brown body. The main feature is a black line on the rear part of the body which follows into the lower lobe of the caudal fin. The fins may be white-tipped. Has a habit of resting at an angle of 45° with a 'tail-down' attitude. Other species of *Thayeria* are distinguished only by differences in the black markings. *Temperature:* 24°C (75°F). *Diet:* all foods. *Breeding:* very prolific, but eggs may be attacked by micro-organisms in the water, because natural waters have a high humus — and hence a low bacterial — content.

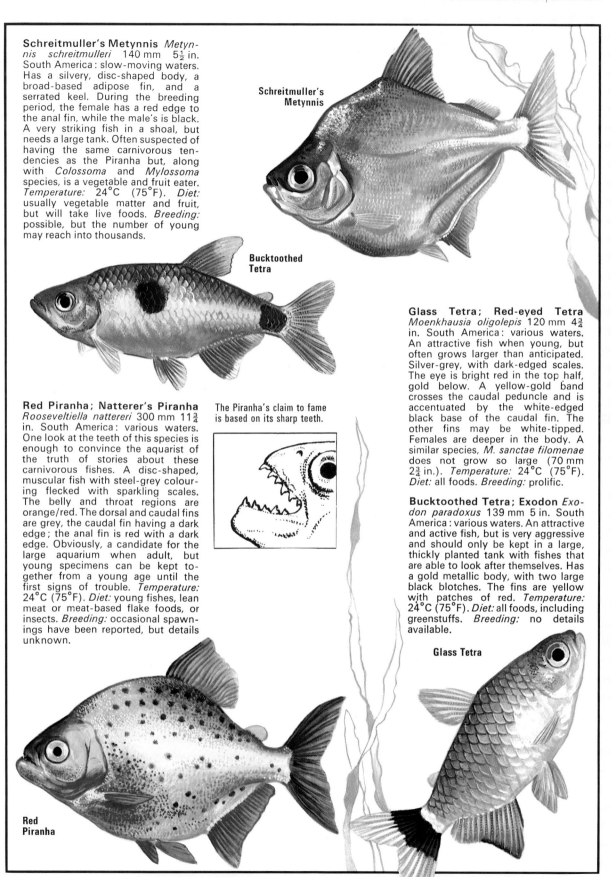

**Schreitmuller's Metynnis** *Metynnis schreitmulleri* 140 mm 5½ in. South America : slow-moving waters. Has a silvery, disc-shaped body, a broad-based adipose fin, and a serrated keel. During the breeding period, the female has a red edge to the anal fin, while the male's is black. A very striking fish in a shoal, but needs a large tank. Often suspected of having the same carnivorous tendencies as the Piranha but, along with *Colossoma* and *Mylossoma* species, is a vegetable and fruit eater. *Temperature:* 24°C (75°F). *Diet:* usually vegetable matter and fruit, but will take live foods. *Breeding:* possible, but the number of young may reach into thousands.

Schreitmuller's Metynnis

Bucktoothed Tetra

**Glass Tetra; Red-eyed Tetra** *Moenkhausia oligolepis* 120 mm 4¾ in. South America : various waters. An attractive fish when young, but often grows larger than anticipated. Silver-grey, with dark-edged scales. The eye is bright red in the top half, gold below. A yellow-gold band crosses the caudal peduncle and is accentuated by the white-edged black base of the caudal fin. The other fins may be white-tipped. Females are deeper in the body. A similar species, *M. sanctae filomenae* does not grow so large (70 mm 2¾ in.). *Temperature:* 24°C (75°F). *Diet:* all foods. *Breeding:* prolific.

**Red Piranha; Natterer's Piranha** *Rooseveltiella nattereri* 300 mm 11¾ in. South America : various waters. One look at the teeth of this species is enough to convince the aquarist of the truth of stories about these carnivorous fishes. A disc-shaped, muscular fish with steel-grey colouring flecked with sparkling scales. The belly and throat regions are orange/red. The dorsal and caudal fins are grey, the caudal fin having a dark edge; the anal fin is red with a dark edge. Obviously, a candidate for the large aquarium when adult, but young specimens can be kept together from a young age until the first signs of trouble. *Temperature:* 24°C (75°F). *Diet:* young fishes, lean meat or meat-based flake foods, or insects. *Breeding:* occasional spawnings have been reported, but details unknown.

The Piranha's claim to fame is based on its sharp teeth.

**Bucktoothed Tetra; Exodon** *Exodon paradoxus* 139 mm 5 in. South America : various waters. An attractive and active fish, but is very aggressive and should only be kept in a large, thickly planted tank with fishes that are able to look after themselves. Has a gold metallic body, with two large black blotches. The fins are yellow with patches of red. *Temperature:* 24°C (75°F). *Diet:* all foods, including greenstuffs. *Breeding:* no details available.

Glass Tetra

Red Piranha

# RELATED SPECIES

The following species may be considered to be closely related to the Characidae and are usually included in the same competitive class by hobbyists. Headstanders are so-called because of their characteristic 'head-down' attitude when resting. Hatchetfishes are hatchet-shaped, deep-bodied fishes that can fly short distances across the water surface, using fins resembling those of the Flying Fish. The Hemiodontidae family are South American fishes distinguished from the Characidae by the lack of teeth in the lower jaw. All Pencilfishes have small mouths and are torpedo-shaped, but not all have adipose fins. They have nocturnal coloration, and the aquarist may be surprised to see them looking different early in the morning.

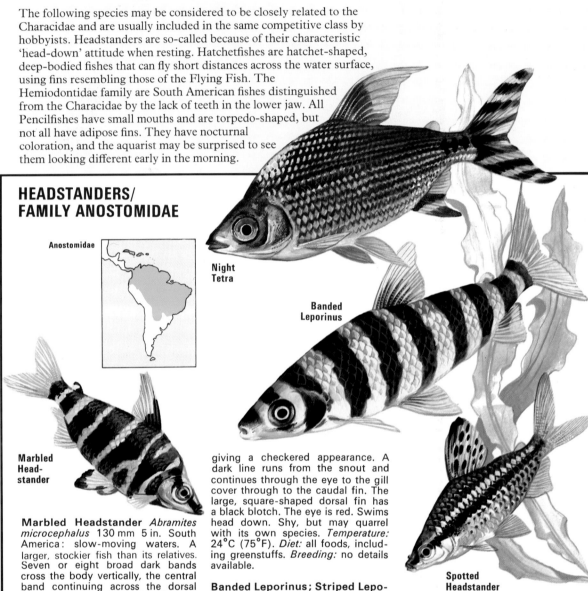

## HEADSTANDERS/ FAMILY ANOSTOMIDAE

Anostomidae

Night Tetra

Banded Leporinus

Marbled Head- stander

Spotted Headstander

**Marbled Headstander** *Abramites microcephalus* 130 mm 5 in. South America: slow-moving waters. A larger, stockier fish than its relatives. Seven or eight broad dark bands cross the body vertically, the central band continuing across the dorsal and ventral fins. The other fins are yellow-brown. The head is very small, and a dark band crosses the eye obliquely. A shy fish, but has a reputation of being a fin-nipper and eater of soft-leaved plants. *Temperature:* 24°C (75°F). *Diet:* worms preferred, and greenstuffs. *Breeding:* no details available.

**Spotted Headstander** *Chilodus punctatus* 75 mm 3 in. South America: slow-moving waters. Not quite so deep-bodied as the Marbled Headstander. The scales have dark spots giving a checkered appearance. A dark line runs from the snout and continues through the eye to the gill cover through to the caudal fin. The large, square-shaped dorsal fin has a black blotch. The eye is red. Swims head down. Shy, but may quarrel with its own species. *Temperature:* 24°C (75°F). *Diet:* all foods, including greenstuffs. *Breeding:* no details available.

**Banded Leporinus; Striped Leporinus** *Leporinus fasciatus* 300 mm 11¾ in. South America: slow-moving waters. Has a long, cylindrical body, yellow in colour and ringed with several dark bands beginning through the eye and ending at the caudal fin. The name Leporinus refers to the shape of the mouth, which is hare-like (*Leporinus* is Latin for a young hare). These fishes are good jumpers, so a glass cover is obligatory. *Temperature:* 24°C (75°F). *Diet:* must contain greenstuffs, otherwise soft-leaved plants will suffer. *Breeding:* no information available.

**Night Tetra; Flagtailed Prochilodus** *Prochilodus insignis* 250 mm 10 in. South America: various waters. Has a silver body with a bluish-green sheen. The caudal and anal fins have horizontal dark blue and white stripes. The dorsal fin may have blue stripes. The other fins are reddish. This fish is an excellent jumper and prefers to be in a shoal. *Temperature:* 24°C (75°F). *Diet:* green foods and some live foods. *Breeding:* not yet bred in the aquarium.

# HATCHETFISHES/ FAMILY GASTEROPELECIDAE

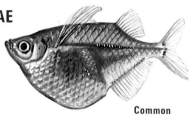

**Common Hatchetfish** *Gasteropelecus sternicla* 65 mm 2½ in. South America: slow-moving waters. A plain, silver fish, with all the physical features of the Marbled Hatchetfish except the marbled patterning. A dark horizontal line extends from behind the gill cover to the caudal fin. The Silver Hatchetfish (*G. levis*) is almost identical, but may have a dark blotch at the base of the dorsal fin. A surface dweller. *Temperature:* 26°C (79°F). *Diet:* insects, floating foods. *Breeding:* not yet bred in the aquarium.

**Marbled Hatchetfish** *Carnegiella strigata* 65 mm 2½ in. South America: slow-moving waters. The fish's deep body shape is necessary to accom-

modate the enlarged muscles that control the movement of the well-developed pectoral fins. A silver fish with attractive marbled patterning below a single, gold horizontal stripe. A glass cover on the tank is essential. *Temperature:* 26°C (79°F). *Diet:* insects and floating foods. *Breeding:* possible, but no information published.

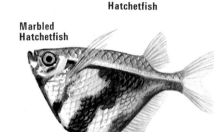

**Common Hatchetfish**

**Marbled Hatchetfish**

**Gasteropelecidae**

---

# FAMILY HEMIODONTIDAE

**Half-lined Hemiodus; Silver Hemiodus; Flying Swallow** *Hemiodopsis* (formerly *Hemiodus*) *semitaeniatus* 200 mm 7¾ in. South America: various waters. A very streamlined, silver fish. A dark spot is situated on the flank between the dorsal and adipose fins. After a gap, a dark line runs into the caudal fin, following a downward direction midway through the lower lobe. A fast swimmer, and loves a shoaling existence. Very attractive when young but grows rapidly. *Temperature:* 24°C (75°F), or slightly lower. *Diet:* all foods. *Breeding:* not yet bred in the aquarium.

**Hemiodontidae**

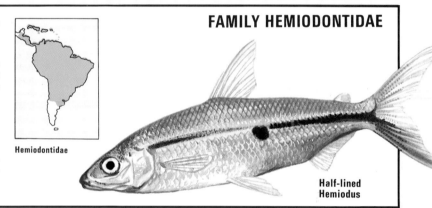

**Half-lined Hemiodus**

---

# PENCILFISHES

**Golden Pencilfish; One-lined Pencilfish** *Nannostomus beckfordi* 50 mm 2 in. South America: jungle streams. Several attempts have been made to sub-divide this species further on a colour-pattern basis. The golden-bodied form with a single, dark horizontal line, red anal fin and

red lower caudal fin has been known as *H. beckfordi anomalus*. The form with a red band alongside the dark band, and red at the base of the caudal fin, may be known as *N. beckfordi aripirangensis*. There is also *N. beckfordi beckfordi*, the Golden Pencilfish, measuring 65 mm (2½ in.) long. Males often spar with each other. *Temperature:* 26°C (79°F). *Diet:* all suitably proportioned foods. *Breeding:* adults are egg eaters. Sometimes water conditions do not favour development of the eggs.

**Dwarf Pencilfish** *Nannostomus marginatus* 38 mm 1½ in. South America: jungle streams. A shorter, stockier fish than other species. The upper half of the body is gold, the lower half silver. A broad dark band, edged above with red, runs from the snout to the caudal fin. Another two black lines parallel this band on either side. The dorsal and anal fins are red, edged in black; the ventral fins are white with a red patch. *Temperature:* 26°C (79°F). *Diet:* all foods. *Breeding:* adults are egg eaters.

**Three-lined Pencilfish** *Nannostomus trifasciatus* 50mm 2in. South America: jungle streams. A 'stretched' version of the Dwarf Pencilfish. Other differences occur in the colour pattern of the fins: the base of the caudal fin has two red patches separated by an over-run of the body colour. The dorsal, anal and ventral fins are clear with red patches. *Temperature:* 26°C (79°F). *Diet:* all foods. *Breeding:* possible, but more difficult than other Pencilfishes, because natural waters are very high in humus content.

**Golden Pencilfish (N. aripirangensis)**

**Dwarf Pencilfish**

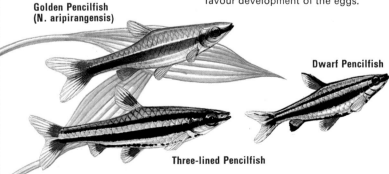

**Three-lined Pencilfish**

# CATFISHES

The sub-Order Siluroidea contains the Catfishes of the aquarium world. With their extended barbels (page 6) around the mouth, the origin of their common group name can be understood. The smaller 'armoured' Catfishes from South America are covered with overlapping large plates instead of the more usual scales, but the Catfishes from Africa have neither, their skin being quite unprotected.

With their flattened bellies, barbels and often large eyes, it is no surprise that these fishes frequent riverbeds searching for food in semi-darkness. Many are nocturnal by nature. In length, they range from 50 mm (2 in) to 600 mm (24 in) or more. Social habits range from peaceful to predatory, and diets from vegetarian to carnivorous. Catfishes are often kept purely as scavengers and subsequently neglected. They should be considered more favourably as the species within this group offer the aquarist a wide range of interests. There are national societies devoted to the study of Catfishes.

**Leopard Corydoras**

## ARMOURED CATFISHES/ FAMILY CALLICHTHYIDAE

**Armoured Catfish**

**Callichthyidae**

**Armoured Catfish; Hassar; Bubblenest Catfish** *Callichthys callichthys* 180 mm 7¼ in. South America: various waters. The body of this species has hardly any taper. Its head is fairly pointed, the barbels well developed. Two rows of overlapping plates cover the body. The caudal fin is rounded, and the first rays of the adipose, dorsal and pectoral fins are thickened into spines and may have a reddish tinge. Because this is a continually rummaging fish, the aquarium should have a filter system capable of dealing with the resulting suspended matter in the water. *Temperature:* 24°C (75°F). *Diet:* all foods. *Breeding:* bubblenest builder among surface leaves of plants.

**Bronze Catfish** *Corydoras aeneus* 75 mm 3 in. South America: various waters. A very popular Catfish, from an equally popular genus. A yellow/reddish/brown body with a dark blue-green metallic sheen on the head and running horizontally along the flanks. The fins are plain and red-brown. Females may be distinguished by the wider cross-section behind the pectoral fins when seen from above. This species often makes a sudden dash to the water surface to gulp air, which is then absorbed in

the gut. It is always foraging for food around the aquarium floor and, as a result, the barbels may be worn away through constant digging. Smooth gravel should be used if a community of *Corydoras* is to be kept. Also, by keeping the fishes well fed, the need for them to dig for food will be obviated. *Temperature:* 24°C (75°F). *Diet:* all foods, but worms relished. *Breeding:* lays eggs on plant leaves or tank glass. Female carries fertilized eggs between ventral fins to selected spawning site. Addition of cooler water to the aquarium may induce spawning.

**Short-bodied Catfish** *Brochis splendens* (*coeruleus*) 76 mm 3 in. South America: slow-moving waters. Has a flat ventral profile and an arched back. The dorsal fin is long-based. The fins are brownish, and the body colour bronze/green. Very similar to the *Corydoras* genus but generally larger; the length of the dorsal fin is conclusive evidence. *Temperature:* 24°C (75°F). *Diet:* all foods; worms relished. *Breeding:* has been bred; probably follows *Corydoras* pattern.

**Bronze Catfish**

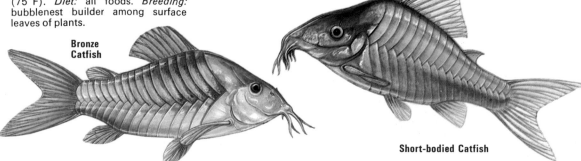

**Short-bodied Catfish**

# SUCKER CATFISHES/ FAMILY LORICARIIDAE

Sucker Catfish

**Sucker Catfish; Plecostomus** *Hypostomus* (formerly *Plecostomus*) *plecostomus* 450 mm 18 in. South America: various waters. The long, wedge-shaped body is covered with bony plates, which may be in three or four ridged layers, instead of only two as in *Corydoras*. The body is dark brown with darker speckles. The dorsal fin is large and sail-like, while the caudal fin is asymmetric, with the lower lobe larger. A shy and retiring fish, but often dashes out for food. An ideal algae-remover that does not damage plants. *Temperature:* 24°C (75°F). *Diet:* all foods, but greenstuffs should predominate. *Breeding:* no details available.

**Midget Sucker Catfish** *Otocinclus affinis* 50 mm 2 in. South America: various waters. This miniature version of the sucking type of Catfish, has a broad, flattened head and tapering body. A dark line runs from the snout into the caudal fin, terminating as a black patch. The dorsal and anal fins are patterned. The back has dark blotches, while the belly is pale. This fish is often seen clinging to aquarium glass. It prefers a shoal of its own kind. *Temperature:* 24°C (75°F). *Diet:* mainly vegetable matter and worms, but will scavenge for scraps. *Breeding:* has been bred in the aquarium, and follows *Corydoras* pattern.

Loricariidae

Midget Sucker Catfish

# AFRICAN CATFISHES/ FAMILY MOCHOKIDAE

**Polka Dot African Catfish** *Synodontis angelicus* 190 mm 7½ in. Africa: slow-moving waters. The young *S. angelicus* is very colourful, being violet with white dots. The adult form is grey with dark blotches. The fins are striped. *Temperature:* 24°C (75°F). *Diet:* live foods, especially worms, and vegetable matter. *Breeding:* not yet bred in the aquarium.

Polka Dot African Catfish

adult

Mochokidae

Synodontis flavitaeniatus

**Synodontis flavitaeniatus** 150 mm 6 in. Africa: various waters. A very striking fish, with a series of light-coloured wavy lines running along the dark body. The fins are patterned with dots. The dorsal fin has a cream leading edge; the caudal fin has cream, dark-bordered edges. *Temperature:* 24°C (75°F). *Diet:* as for *S. angelicus*. *Breeding:* has been bred in the aquarium, but details unknown.

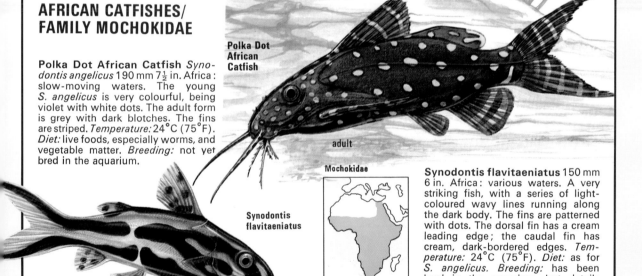

# GLASS CATFISHES/ FAMILY SILURIDAE

**Glass Catfish** *Kryptopterus bicirrhis* 90 mm 3½ in. Indonesia, Thailand: shallow waters. Has a totally transparent body with the internal organs enclosed in a silvery sac. The anal fin is very long, while the dorsal fin is reduced to a single ray. The caudal fin is forked and often asymmetric. Swims at an oblique angle, with the tail down. A not too active fish that prefers a peaceful tank and the company of a shoal. A similar species is the slightly larger Poor Man's Glass Catfish (*K. macrocephalus*). *Temperature:* 24°C (75°C). *Diet:* live foods preferred. *Breeding:* not yet bred in the aquarium.

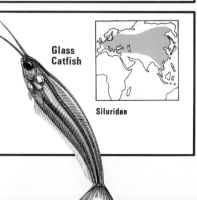

Glass Catfish

Siluridae

# EGGLAYING TOOTH-CARPS/KILLIFISHES

The Egglaying Toothcarps comprise mainly the so-called 'annual' fishes whose natural watery habitat completely dries up every year, thus killing the fishes. However, before this event occurs, the adult fishes lay their fertilized eggs in the mud of the stream bed, where they survive the rest of the dry season in a dormant state. The onset of the rainy season refills the stream bed and the eggs hatch. The fish then have to mature and spawn in their turn before the weather cycle is repeated.

These fishes are extremely colourful, but they require slightly different conditions from those needed by the usual 'tropical' species. They do not need such a high water temperature and, because of their aggressiveness, are not suitable for a mixed community collection. Killifishes are usually kept in 'peaty' water which has an acid reaction; its amber coloration sets off the colours of the fishes perfectly. They prefer dimly lit aquaria, and this is easily provided by heavily planting the tank.

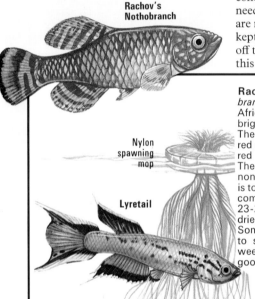

Rachov's Nothobranch

Nylon spawning mop

Lyretail

**Rachov's Nothobranch** *Nothobranchius rachovi* 50 mm 2 in. East Africa: pools. A very colourful fish, bright-red with light blue specklings. The dorsal and anal fins are blue with red stripes; the caudal fin is blue with red patterning and a black rear edge. The female is quite drab and shows none of her partner's colours. The fish is too aggressive to be kept in a mixed community collection. *Temperature:* 23-26°C (72-79°F). *Diet:* live and dried foods. *Breeding:* buries its eggs. Sometimes female may be too small to spawn. Eggs stored at least six weeks. Fry mature in 6-8 weeks with good feeding.

**Steel-blue Aphyosemion** *Aphyosemion gardneri* 75 mm 3 in. Nigeria, Cameroon: streams. This species has several colour variants. The body colour is blue, with red markings extending into the fins. The dorsal and caudal fins have a horizontal red line parallel to the edge of the fin. The Blue variety has a white edging to the fins outside the red line, whereas the Yellow variety has a yellow margin. Many 'new' species are often found to be only regional colour variations of an already existing species. *Temperature:* 18-22°C (65-72°F). *Diet:* live and dried foods. *Breeding:* a ready mop spawner.

## FAMILY CYPRINODONTIDAE

**Lyretail; Lyre-tailed Panchax; Cape Lopez Lyretail** *Aphyosemion australe* 65 mm 2½ in. West Africa, Gabon: coastal marshes. The cylindrical body is red/brown covered with dark red speckles. The red dorsal fin has white extensions, while the anal fin has a red and green border, with white extensions. The caudal fin has yellow edges, with white 'lyretail' extensions; the centre section is blue, with red patterning and a dark rear edge. Females are a paler brown, without extensions to their fins. *Temperature:* 18-22°C (65-72°F). *Diet:* insect larvae, worms (fed to the fish in floating worm feeders), and dried foods. *Breeding:* removable nylon mops are used as a spawning medium by the fishes. Eggs can be transferred from the mops and stored in shallow water in plastic dishes until hatching occurs in two to four weeks.

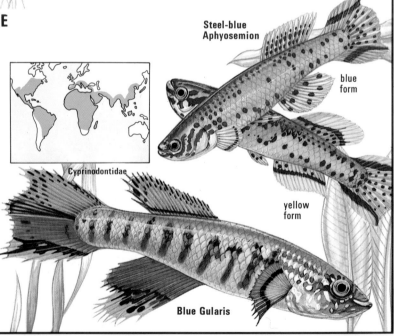

Steel-blue Aphyosemion

blue form

yellow form

Cyprinodontidae

Blue Gularis

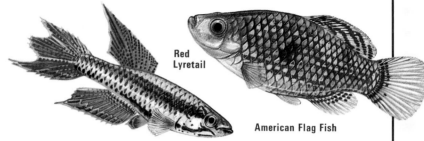

**Blue Gularis** *Aphyosemion sjoe-stedti* 110 mm 4¼ in. Nigeria, Cameroon: marshy areas. The green-blue/brown body has a red patch running from the snout to mid-body. Vertical red bands cross the rear half of the body. The anal fin is gold with a blue and red edging. The dorsal fin has a red base and red flecking. The large caudal fin has an orange centre section extended to the same length as the outer rays; the upper lobe is green-blue with a red marking; the lower lobe is blue with red markings. *Temperature:* 18-22°C (65-72°F). *Diet:* live and dried foods. *Breeding:* bottom spawner in peat or non-floating mops. Eggs may be stored nearly dry for a month or so before being re-immersed for hatching to occur.

Red Lyretail

American Flag Fish

**Red Lyretail** *Aphyosemion bivitt-tatum* 60 mm 2¼ in. West Africa, Cameroon: streams. The purplish body has a dark line running from the snout into the flanks. The scales are edged in violet or red, giving a glittering appearance. The ventral, pectoral and anal fins are red/orange with blue and red edgings. The dorsal fin is red/gold, with specklings. The caudal fin is a mixture of purple, green and orange, with a blue and red edge. *Temperature:* 18-22°C (65-72°F). *Diet:* live and dried foods. *Breeding:* mop spawner.

**American Flag Fish** *Jordanella floridae* 70 mm 2¾ in. Florida, Yucatán (Mexico): various waters. The stocky, blue-green body has a red, reticulated pattern which extends into the fins of the male. There is also a dark blotch on the flank below the front edge of the dorsal fin. The female does not have red patterning but carries a light-edged dark blotch at the rear edge of the dorsal fin. This fish may be pugnacious. *Temperature:* 18-25°C (65-76°F). *Diet:* live and dried foods. Reputed to eat blue-green algae, and generally appreciates some vegetable matter. *Breeding:* lays eggs in depression in gravel. Male guards eggs and fry; female should be removed after spawning. Author's fish spawned in aquarium plants (*Cabomba*) in midwater, and eggs repeatedly affected by fungus until methylene blue was added to water. Hatching takes 10 days.

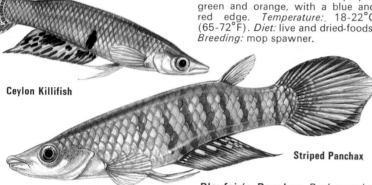

Ceylon Killifish

Striped Panchax

**Ceylon Killifish** *Aplocheilus dayi* 70 mm 2¾ in. Southern India, Sri Lanka: streams. Has a cylindrical body and pike-like head. The gold-green body has some dark dots on the flanks. The scales appear to be outlined individually. The dorsal fin is set well back and, like the anal fin, may be marked with dark streaks. The caudal fin is round, with a red margin and markings. *Temperature:* 23-26°C (73-78°F). *Diet:* live and dried foods. *Breeding:* may prefer peat fibre as an alternative to mops. Eggs hatch in two weeks.

**Striped Panchax** *Aplocheilus lineatus* 100 mm 4 in. Southern India, Sri Lanka: streams. Has a golden brown body. The golden scales are redotted on the front half of the body and there are vertical, dark half bands across the rear of the body. The female has broader and more numerous dark stripes. The dorsal fin is gold with white dots. The anal fin has a long base with a red edge. The female dorsal fin has a dark spot at the base. The ventral fins are elongated in the male. The caudal fin has a red edging along the top and bottom. *Temperature:* 23-26°C (73-78°F). *Diet:* live and dried foods. *Breeding:* mop spawner.

**Playfair's Panchax** *Pachypanchax playfairi* 76 mm 3 in. East Africa, Malagasy, Seychelles: various waters. The cylindrical body is gold-brown with rows of red dots. The fins are blue-yellow with a dark edging and some red dots. The dorsal fin is set well back. A feature of this fish is that the scales are raised, standing out from the body in a manner which suggest the onset of the condition dropsy. *Temperature:* 24°C (75°F). *Diet:* live and dried foods. *Breeding:* mop spawner. Often spawns in a community tank, and the young fry may be rescued from floating plants such as *Riccia* when noticed.

**Clown Killi; Rocket Panchax** *Pseudoepiplatys annulatus* 45 mm 1¾ in. West Africa: streams. A miniature Killifish, with a light brown cylindrical body ringed by four broad, dark bands. The dorsal fin has bright-red front rays. The caudal fin has an orange-red centre section which extends to a point with light-blue bordering areas. When seen against a dark background the fish may resemble a rocket in flight, hence the common name. This species may be more delicate than other Killifishes. *Temperature:* 24°C (75°F). *Diet:* live and dried foods. *Breeding:* mop spawner. Fry very small.

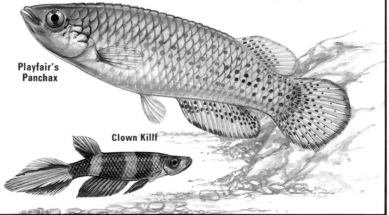

Playfair's Panchax

Clown Killi

# LIVEBEARING FISHES

This group of fishes is unique in that rather than being released into the water as eggs the young develop inside the body of the female and are born as small, free-swimming fishes. As many as 200 young may be born in each brood and it is possible for the females of some species to deliver successive broods without a repeat mating with the male. It is easy to distinguish between the sexes of many livebearing fishes as the males have a specially modified anal fin called the *gonopodium*. This is used to transfer sperm into the female during mating.

Many colour strains of livebearers seen in dealers are the result of 'line-breeding' programmes by hobbyists, as such colour patternings or fin shapes do not occur in nature. Livebearing fishes are mainly native to Central and South America, but some may be found in Asia. Many of these fishes are happy to eat green algae, and some vegetable matter should be regularly provided for them.

## FAMILY GOODEIDAE

**Ameca splendens** Male 75 mm 3 in. Central America: various waters. At first sight, does not appear to have the sexual differences of a livebearing fish: the anal fin is not completely modified into a gonopodium; only the first few rays are slightly separated from the anal fin to form a primitive reproductive organ. Has a silvery blue-grey body covered in dark brown speckles, which are more concentrated in a broad band along the flanks. Males have less distinct specklings but have a bright yellow band on the rear edge of the caudal fin. Species within the Goodeidae family are often aggressive. *Temperature:* 24°C (75°F). *Diet:* live and dried foods. *Breeding:* gestation period may be 6 to 8 weeks. Females cannot produce successive broods from a single mating. Young draw nourishment from the female via a placenta before birth.

Orange-tailed Goodea *Xenotoca eiseni* Male 65 mm 2½ in; female slightly larger. Central Mexico: various waters. A very colourful fish. The stocky body is metallic turquoise blue, with an orange caudal fin in the male. Females have a silvery yellow body with plain fins. An aggressive fish. *Temperature:* 24°C (75°F). *Diet:* all foods. *Breeding:* prolific, but ratio of males to females in brood may be low.

Orange-tailed Goodea

male

Ameca splendens

female

## FAMILY HEMIRHAMPHIDAE

**Half Beak; Wrestling Half Beak** *Dermogenys pusillus* 65 mm 2½ in. Far East: various waters. Has a long cylindrical body, with the lower jaw extended far beyond the upper, so that the fish is forced to take food from the surface. The anal fin in males is not developed into a rod-like gonopodium but is similar to the fin development in the Goodeidae genera. The aquarium should be well-planted around the glass as the fish, if frightened, may swim into it and damage the lower jaw. A golden brown colour, with some red in the yellow fins. *Temperature:* will tolerate a wide range, from 20-30°C (68-86°F). *Diet:* insects, floating foods. *Breeding:* temperature should be 25°C (76°F) or higher, as low temperatures may result in deformed fry. Females will eat their own young, so shallow water and a well-planted nursery tank essential. Salt may be added to the aquarium but is not vital.

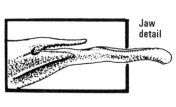

Jaw detail

Half Beak

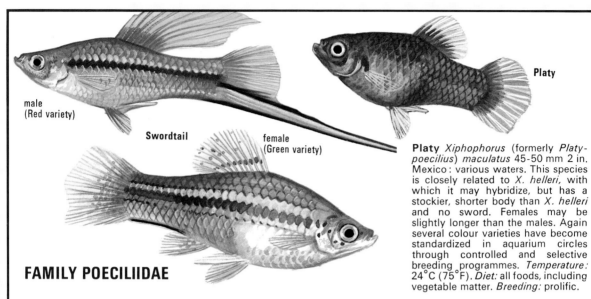

male
(Red variety)

Swordtail

female
(Green variety)

Platy

# FAMILY POECILIIDAE

**Platy** *Xiphophorus* (formerly *Platy-poecilius*) *maculatus* 45-50 mm 2 in. Mexico : various waters. This species is closely related to *X. helleri*, with which it may hybridize, but has a stockier, shorter body than *X. helleri* and no sword. Females may be slightly longer than the males. Again several colour varieties have become standardized in aquarium circles through controlled and selective breeding programmes. *Temperature:* 24°C (75°F). *Diet:* all foods, including vegetable matter. *Breeding:* prolific.

**Sailfin Molly** *Poecilia* (formerly *Mollienisia*) *latipinna* Male 100 mm 4 in; female 110 mm 4½ in. Mexico: various waters, including those affected by tides. The body is olive-green with a yellow overcast; the scales may appear to be iridescent. Several rows of dark dots run along the body, and the belly often has dark transverse bars. The male fish has a very tall dorsal fin. A jet-black variety has been established in the aquarium, and gold and albino strains have become common in recent years. A similar species, *P. velifera* (also known as the Sailfin Molly), grows slightly larger. All Mollies benefit by the addition of salt to the aquarium water. *Temperature:* 24°C (75°F). *Diet:* very fond of greenstuffs, but takes all foods. *Breeding:* usual livebearer pattern, but females become nervous when gravid and should not be moved when about to give birth, otherwise premature births will occur resulting in undeveloped young.

**Swordtail** *Xiphophorus helleri* 100 mm 4 in. Mexico: various waters. An easily recognized species : males have a sword-like extension to the bottom edge of the caudal fin. Females may be slightly deeper in the body and a little longer. Natural species are greenish, with a reddish horizontal stripe and a green sword edged with black. Aquarium varieties include Reds, Red-eyed Reds, Wagtail (coloured body, black fins), Green, Tuxedo and Wiesbaden. These are recognized internationally. Occasionally sex reversal occurs (female to male). *Temperature:* 24°C (75°F). *Diet:* all foods, including vegetable matter. *Breeding:* prolific; broods of over 250 young have been reported.

**Guppy; Millions Fish** *Poecilia* (formerly *Lebistes*) *reticulata* Male 28-32 mm 1-1¼ in; females 65 mm 2½ in. Trinidad : various waters. A well-known species. No two males are ever exactly alike; the females are much larger and do not share the males' rainbow colours. Genetic experimentation by hobbyists has resulted in many colours and finnage shapes becoming internationally recognized standards. Several specialist groups exist solely for the Guppy fancier. Serious breeders separate the sexes as soon as they are recognizable to prevent unwanted broods. *Temperature:* 24°C (75°F). *Diet:* all foods. *Breeding:* very prolific. Females should be given a separate, well-planted tank in which to give birth.

male

Guppy

female

Humpbacked
Limia

Mosquitofish

Sailfin
Molly

**Mosquitofish; Dwarf Top Minnow; Dwarf Livebearer** *Heterandria formosa* Male 20 mm ¾ in; female nearly twice as big. Central America : various waters. One of the smallest livebearers and not readily

recognized as being related to *H. bimaculata.* The body is brown, with a horizontal dark line and white belly. Some transverse dark bars cross the back down to the horizontal line. The dorsal and anal fins carry dark marks. *Temperature:* 24°C (75°F), or slightly lower. *Diet:* live and dried foods, including vegetable matter. *Breeding:* young produced over a period of days; will eat own young, so a well-planted nursery tank is recommended.

**Humpbacked Limia** *Poecilia* (formerly *Limia*) *nigrofasciata* Male 50 mm 2 in; female 70 mm 2¾ in. Haiti: lakes. Has a yellow/brown body with dark-edged scales and several transverse dark stripes. The dorsal fin is speckled. Males have high, arched backs and may become darker with age. The sexes can be identified only when almost full-grown. A peaceful fish. *Temperature:* 24°C (75°F). *Diet:* all foods, including vegetable matter. *Breeding:* usual pattern.

# LABYRINTH FISHES

Fishes in this family get their common name from a labyrinthine organ in the head which allows them to breathe atmospheric air if necessary. Another distinguishing feature of this group is the breeding pattern: the majority of the fishes are bubblenest builders. The nests are made of saliva-coated bubbles blown by the male, into which the fertilized eggs are placed following the nuptial embrace beneath the nest. The fry are guarded and kept within the vicinity of the nest by the male.

Labyrinth fishes are native to Africa and Asia. The Asian species have long, filament-like ventral fins, which can be extended in front of the fish at will. These have taste cells at their tips so that the fish can find food in the often dark waters of its natural habitat. With one or two exceptions, the Anabantidae is a peaceful family and provides welcome additions to the community tank.

Anabantidae

## LABYRINTH FISHES/ FAMILY ANABANTIDAE

male

female

**Siamese Fighting Fish**

**Honey Gourami** *Colisa chuna* 45 mm 1¾ in. India: various waters. The smallest of the genus. The body is compressed laterally and is honey-brown in colour. Males have a purple/green coloration to the head and breast, which extends diagonally across the red-edged anal fin during the spawning period. The dorsal fin has a yellow/gold top edge. The ventral fins may be red. The female is a uniform brown, with a dark horizontal stripe along the flanks. *Temperature:* 24°C (75°F). *Diet:* all foods. *Breeding:* fry fairly small and need microscopic first foods – that is, green water and infusoria.

**Siamese Fighting Fish** *Betta splendens* 60 mm 2¼ in. Thailand: standing waters. This fish has a reputation for the pugnacity of the males, and the likely results of combats between them are the subject of many wagers in their native country. The body is cylindrical, with very flowing fins, particularly the dorsal, anal and caudal fins. The ventral fins are very elongated and narrow. When males confront each other, the gill covers are raised and the fins spread in a threatening manner. The females, which are not aggressive, do not have such elongated fins and are less colourful. Many colour strains exist in the 'man-made' varieties: the Cambodian strain has a light-coloured body with dark-coloured fins. *Temperature:* 24°C (75°F). *Diet:* all foods. *Breeding:* fairly prolific, but space has to be found for the separate accommodation of male fishes from the brood; luckily, in a space-heated fish house, small jars will suffice.

**Dwarf Gourami** *Colisa lalia* 60 mm 2½ in. India: various waters. The brilliantly coloured males have a basic body colour of blue/grey overlaid with numerous, zig-zag, slanting, bright-red stripes. The ventral fins are red. The other fins are highly decorated. The females are far less striking in colour. They are grey/brown with only faint turquoise markings and semi-patterned fins. The males are aggressive at breeding time to any other fish in the vicinity. They will also attack the female if she is considered not ready for spawning. *Temperature:* 24°C (75°F). *Diet:* all foods. *Breeding:* bubblenest construction includes pieces of aquatic plants. Male very possessive and protective of nest and fry. Female best removed after spawning. Fry very small, so microscopic food a necessity. Ratio of males to females in brood low.

Chocolate Gourami

**Chocolate Gourami** *Sphaerichthys osphromenoides* 60 mm 2¼ in. Malaysia: various waters. A challenging fish which is difficult to keep. The chocolate-brown body has cream/gold transverse stripes which merge into a pale band along the ventral contour. The dorsal and anal fin is light brown. No sex differences are identifiable. This fish is prone to diseases and is also sensitive to the cures used to counteract them. *Temperature:* 28°C (81°F). *Diet:* insect larvae and live foods. *Breeding:* problematical. May be nest builder and/or mouthbrooder depending on habitat.

Honey Gourami

Dwarf Gourami

24

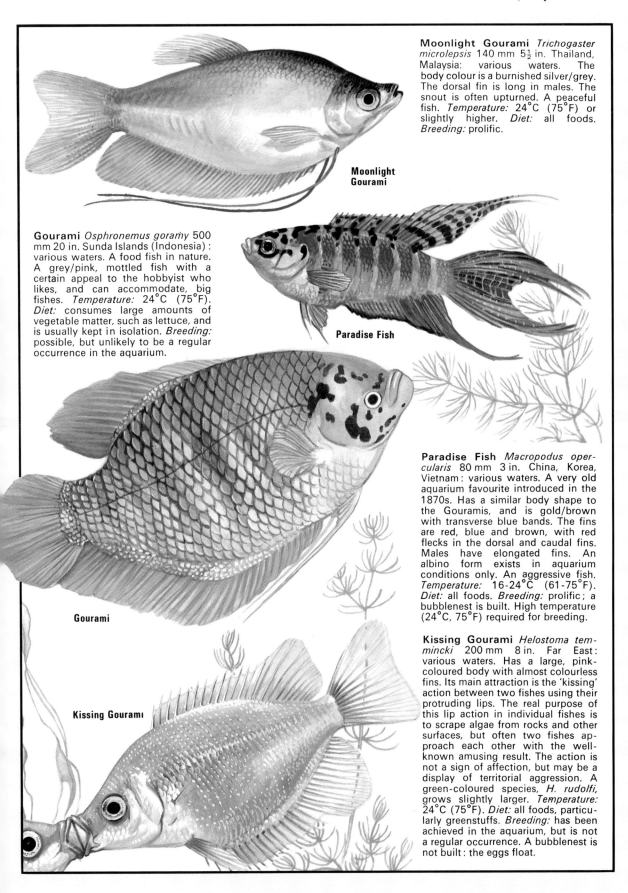

**Moonlight Gourami** *Trichogaster microlepis* 140 mm 5½ in. Thailand, Malaysia: various waters. The body colour is a burnished silver/grey. The dorsal fin is long in males. The snout is often upturned. A peaceful fish. *Temperature:* 24°C (75°F) or slightly higher. *Diet:* all foods. *Breeding:* prolific.

**Moonlight Gourami**

**Gourami** *Osphronemus goramy* 500 mm 20 in. Sunda Islands (Indonesia) : various waters. A food fish in nature. A grey/pink, mottled fish with a certain appeal to the hobbyist who likes, and can accommodate, big fishes. *Temperature:* 24°C (75°F). *Diet:* consumes large amounts of vegetable matter, such as lettuce, and is usually kept in isolation. *Breeding:* possible, but unlikely to be a regular occurrence in the aquarium.

**Paradise Fish**

**Gourami**

**Kissing Gourami**

**Paradise Fish** *Macropodus opercularis* 80 mm 3 in. China, Korea, Vietnam: various waters. A very old aquarium favourite introduced in the 1870s. Has a similar body shape to the Gouramis, and is gold/brown with transverse blue bands. The fins are red, blue and brown, with red flecks in the dorsal and caudal fins. Males have elongated fins. An albino form exists in aquarium conditions only. An aggressive fish. *Temperature:* 16-24°C (61-75°F). *Diet:* all foods. *Breeding:* prolific ; a bubblenest is built. High temperature (24°C, 75°F) required for breeding.

**Kissing Gourami** *Helostoma temmincki* 200 mm 8 in. Far East: various waters. Has a large, pink-coloured body with almost colourless fins. Its main attraction is the 'kissing' action between two fishes using their protruding lips. The real purpose of this lip action in individual fishes is to scrape algae from rocks and other surfaces, but often two fishes approach each other with the well-known amusing result. The action is not a sign of affection, but may be a display of territorial aggression. A green-coloured species, *H. rudolfi*, grows slightly larger. *Temperature:* 24°C (75°F). *Diet:* all foods, particularly greenstuffs. *Breeding:* has been achieved in the aquarium, but is not a regular occurrence. A bubblenest is not built : the eggs float.

# CICHLIDS

These perch-like fishes are considered to be among the more highly evolved species of fishes. The best evidence of this is perhaps the amount of parental care shown by the adult fishes when breeding. A pair of adult fishes will often form a 'pair-bond' which lasts for years. Generally the male of the species has the longer fins and the brighter colours, although in some species the female is just as colourful as the male.

American and Asian Cichlids live in a wide range of natural habitats in rivers and lakes. Most are fairly large and may be aggressive at times.

The majority of African Cichlids inhabit the Rift Valley lakes and are spectacularly coloured. These fishes are from naturally hard waters, unlike their South American relatives, and may relish algae or other vegetable matter in their diet. Some are mouthbrooding, and all appreciate a tank furnished with hideaways.

**Cichlidae**

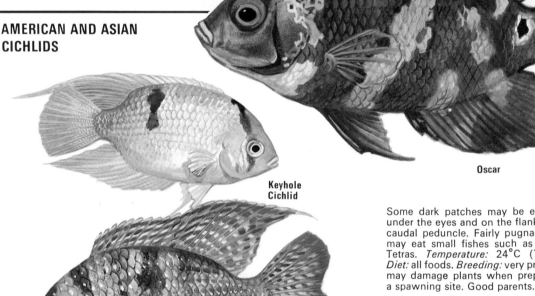

## AMERICAN AND ASIAN CICHLIDS

**Keyhole Cichlid**

**Blue Acara**

**Oscar**

Some dark patches may be evident under the eyes and on the flanks and caudal peduncle. Fairly pugnacious; may eat small fishes such as Neon Tetras. *Temperature:* 24°C (75°F). *Diet:* all foods. *Breeding:* very prolific; may damage plants when preparing a spawning site. Good parents.

**Oscar** *Astronotus ocellatus* 300 mm 12 in. South America, widely distributed. A large fish whose adult coloration is quite different from its juvenile form. The black and white, marbled colour of the young turns to an olive-brown, mottled with red speckles and rust-coloured patches. The head is blunt and the mouth very large. A gold-edged, black blotch is present on the caudal peduncle. The attraction of the adult fish is that it becomes very tame: it takes food from its owner's hands and is reputed even to enjoy a friendly stroke. Needs a large tank. *Temperature:* 24°C (75°F). *Diet:* a hearty eater of meaty foods, but will eat almost anything. Because of its large appetite, the tank soon soon becomes dirty with the fish's droppings and partial changes of water should be done frequently. *Breeding:* very prolific.

**Keyhole Cichlid** *Aequidens maronii* 100 mm 4 in. Guyana, Surinam, French Guiana: rivers. Not a very colourful fish, the body colour varying from cream to dark brown. The main characteristic is the keyhole-shaped blotch on the flanks, which is quite recognizable in young specimens but tends to spread into a less distinct pattern with maturity. A dark, oblique stripe runs through the eye. A peaceful, even shy fish, which can live to over seven years in the aquarium.

*Temperature:* 24°C (75°F). *Diet:* all foods. *Breeding:* not difficult, but fry may be harder to raise than those of other *Aequidens* species.

**Blue Acara** *Aequidens pulcher* (formerly *latifrons*) 180 mm 7 in. Venezuela, Colombia, Panama: rivers. An old-established aquarium favourite. A similar coloured Cichlid, *A. cuviceps,* is smaller with less blue streaking over the head and less specking on the body and fins.

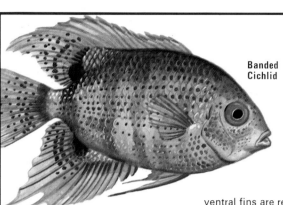

Banded
Cichlid

Brown
Discus

Firemouth

**Banded Cichlid** *Cichlasoma severum*
20 mm 8 in. Central America and
Amazon basin. A stocky, deep-bodied
fish, green-brown in colour. Young
specimens have several vertical,
dark bands crossing the body, but
these bands fade with maturity.
*Temperature:* 24°C (75°F). *Diet:* all
foods. *Breeding:* fairly prolific, especially from naturally selected parents.

**Pike Cichlid** *Crenicichla lepidota*
230 mm 9 in. Central America: various
waters. A predatory fish, with a
pointed head and large mouth. The
powerfully built, torpedo-shaped
body is blue-grey with a speckling of
silver-white dots. A dark line runs
from the snout horizontally along the
body to a light-ringed dark spot in
the caudal fin. This fish cannot be
kept with other fishes, and is even
aggressive towards its own kind. The
tank should be large enough to
accommodate rocky hiding places.
*Temperature:* 24°C (75°F). *Diet:*
a voracious feeder, all foods being
literally snapped up. *Breeding:* deposits eggs in pits in the gravel and
guards them.

**Brown Discus; Pompadour Fish**
*Symphysodon aequifasciata axelrodi*
150 mm 6 in. Amazon basin. A slow-
moving and graceful fish with a
disc-shaped body and dorsal and
anal fins that follow the body contour.
The body colour is brown, with eight
or nine dark, vertical bands crossing
the body. Blue-green wavy lines
cover the head, dorsal and anal fins.
The dorsal and anal fins also have a
dark band running through them,
following the outline of the body.
The edges of these fins and the

ventral fins are red. This genus is very
demanding in its requirements: soft
water, regular replacement of a proportion with water of similar composition, and high temperature. *Temperature:* 28-32°C (82-91°F). *Diet:* live
foods; beef heart and some dried
foods taken. *Breeding:* spawns in
similar manner to the Angelfish; fry,
when free swimming, feed from
special mucus developed on parents'
bodies; it is consequently very difficult
to raise the young away from the
adult fishes.

**Angelfish** *Pterophyllum scalare*
(*eimekei*) 110 mm 4½ in. Amazon
basin. Perhaps the most widely
recognized aquarium fish, apart from
the Goldfish. The disc-shaped body
is very compressed laterally. The high
dorsal fin is equally matched by the
long anal fin. The caudal fin is
triangular, and the ventral fins have
elongated, bony rays. A slow-moving,
graceful fish. Colour varieties include
the original natural silver fish with
four black vertical dark bars; and the
aquarium-developed All-Black, Half-
Black, Marbled, Blushing and Gold
varieties. Similarly, the finnage has
been further developed into Lace and
Veiltail forms. This fish appreciates
deep tanks and tall, grass-like plants
such as *Vallisneria* and *Sagittaria*,
among which it can glide. Usually
peaceful until large, when small,
colourful fishes might be regarded as
a likely meal. *Temperature:* 24°C
(75°F), slightly higher for breeding.
*Diet:* all foods, especially insect
larvae. *Breeding:* deposits eggs on
near-vertical surfaces which are pre-
cleaned. Sites may be plant leaves or
pieces of slate. Eggs are fanned,
guarded and moved to newer, prepared sites until hatching occurs.

**Firemouth** *Cichlasoma meeki* 150
mm 6 in. Central America (Guatemala,
Yucatán). The head of this species is
pointed, with a steep forehead. The
body is deep and laterally compressed.
A gold-edged black spot is present on
the gill cover, and a black patch
occurs on the flank below the dorsal
fin. Some dark, vertical bars may
be present depending on the fish's
mood. The dorsal fin may be
elongated into filaments in the male.
The male's throat and belly region
is crimson red, and this is intensified
in the breeding period. This fish
may be guilty of occasional digging,
but is generally peaceful and less
shy than *C. festivum. Temperature:*
24°C (75°F). *Diet:* all foods. *Breeding:*
fairly prolific.

Angelfish

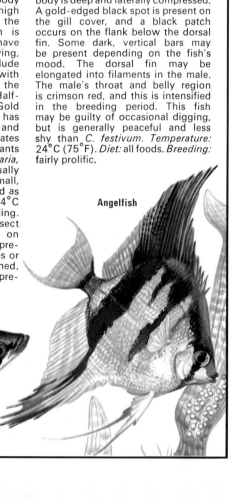

Pike
Cichlid

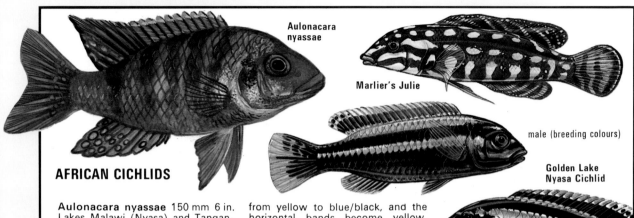

Aulonacara
nyassae

Marlier's Julie

male (breeding colours)

Golden Lake
Nyasa Cichlid

female

# AFRICAN CICHLIDS

**Aulonacara nyassae** 150 mm 6 in. Lakes Malawi (Nyasa) and Tanganyika. Has an elongated, fairly deep body. Young males and females have brown bodies with several vertical dark bars, but mature males are deep royal blue with a red/gold suffusion on the flanks, which are crossed with dark bars. The fins are blue; the dorsal fin is edged with pale blue and the caudal fin has dark blue/black streaks. A peaceful fish, but caves and hiding places must be provided in a reasonably sized tank. *Temperature:* 24°C (75°F). *Diet:* all foods. *Breeding:* mouthbrooder.

**Golden Lake Nyasa Cichlid** *Melanochromis* (formerly *Pseudotropheus*) *auratus* 100 mm 4 in. Lake Malawi (Nyasa). Has an elongated, bright-yellow body. Two black bands, edged on either side with white, run along the back from the snout to the base of the caudal fin. The dorsal and caudal fins have black patterning; the anal fin is plain yellow. During the breeding period, the male changes from yellow to blue/black, and the horizontal bands become yellow, edged with white. The dorsal fin turns to light yellow/blue; the caudal fin becomes dark with a yellow edge, and the anal fin dark with a white edge. This fish may be aggressive and should be given a large tank with many hiding places. *Temperature:* 24°C (75°F). *Diet:* all foods, including vegetable matter. *Breeding:* mouthbrooder.

**Fuelleborn's Cichlid** *Labeotropheus fuelleborni* 180 mm 7 in. Lake Malawi (Nyasa). The elongated, blue body has several darker blue, vertical bands. Two dark bands cross the snout. All the fins, except the pectorals, have red areas, and the anal fin carries 2 to 4 oval, dark-edged yellow spots. There is a dark mark immediately behind the gill opening. Females are generally blue, but some are orange, peppered with black dots and blotches. The mouth is somewhat underslung, as this species browses on algae-covered surfaces.

*Temperature:* 24°C (75°F). *Diet:* all foods, including greenstuffs. *Breeding:* mouthbrooder.

**Marlier's Julie** *Julidochromis marlieri* 110 mm 4½ in. A very smart-looking fish with a cylindrical, cream body with dark markings that link up to form a latticed pattern. The long-based dorsal fin has light blue edging and flecking. The light blue anal fin has a dark edge. The caudal fin is rounded and has a dark edge bordered with light blue. Hard water must be provided, with rocky retreats. *Temperature:* 24°C (75°F). *Diet:* all foods, including algae and lettuce. *Breeding:* deposits eggs on inside roof of cave or on undersides of rocks.

**Jewel Cichlid** *Hemichromis bimaculatus* 120 mm 4¾ in. Throughout Africa. An aggressive fish, whose behaviour is redeemed by its brilliant coloration and exceptional conduct as a parent. The reddish-brown body has an overlay of shining blue-green speckles. There is a black spot midway along the flanks and another on the gill cover. The fins are also speckled. At breeding time both sexes change to a brilliant red colour. This species has often been used in laboratory tests to evaluate fish intellect. *Temperature:* 24°C (75°F). *Diet:* all foods. *Breeding:* usual Cichlid pattern; open site spawner.

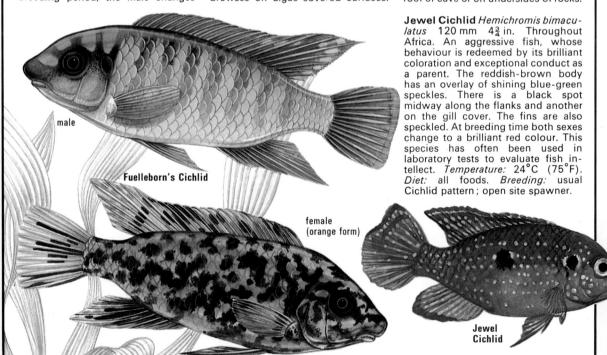

male

Fuelleborn's Cichlid

female
(orange form)

Jewel
Cichlid

Julie

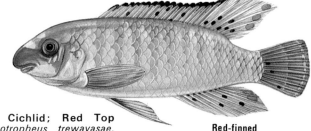

Red-finned Cichlid

**Julie** *Julidochromis ornatus* 80 mm 3¼ in. Lake Tanganyika. The yellow body has three dark, horizontal bands. There is a dark spot at the base of the yellow caudal fin, which has a dark edge. The dorsal and anal fins are yellow, with black and light-coloured edgings. *Temperature:* 24°C (75°F). *Diet* and *Breeding:* as for *J. marlieri.*

**Red-finned Cichlid; Red Top Zebra** *Labeotropheus trewavasae.* 150 mm 6 in. Lake Malawi (Nyasa). The body is blue, with darker, vertical bands. The dorsal fin is bright red/ orange. The caudal fin has some red speckling, and the anal fin bears 2 to 3 yellow spots. Females are usually blue, but speckled versions occur as in *L. fuelleborni.* *Temperature:* 24°C (75°F). *Diet* and *Breeding:* as for *L. fuelleborni.*

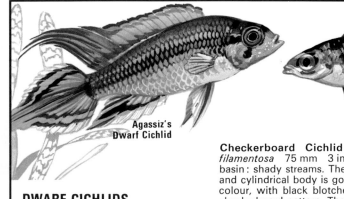

Agassiz's Dwarf Cichlid

Checkerboard Cichlid

# DWARF CICHLIDS

**Agassiz's Dwarf Cichlid** *Apistogramma agassizi* 70 mm 2¾ in. Amazon basin: shady streams. The elongated body is brown, with a blue sheen in the male and dark-edged scales. The caudal fin of the male is spear-shaped, with a white outline inside the dark margin. The long-based dorsal fin is edged in red and white. Females are more drab, with a yellow-brown body that has a dark, horizontal line running along the flanks and a slanting, dark line through the eye. The caudal fin is rounded. In general, females of the *Apistogramma* genus (except for the following species) are similar and difficult to identify. *Temperature:* 24°C (75°F), or slightly higher. *Diet:* all foods. *Breeding:* secretive; deposits eggs in caves or upturned flowerpots.

Golden-eyed Dwarf Cichlid

**Checkerboard Cichlid** *Crenicara filamentosa* 75 mm 3 in. Amazon basin: shady streams. The elongated and cylindrical body is gold-green in colour, with black blotches giving a checkerboard pattern. The outer rays of the caudal fin are extended into filaments; the fins are more elongated in the male. A similar species. *C. maculata,* does not have the filaments on the fins. A rather shy fish that tends to creep around the base of the aquarium. It is sensitive to water conditions, so a clean tank is necessary. *Temperature:* 24°C (75°F). *Diet:* all foods, particularly worms. *Breeding:* deposits eggs in prepared sites or in crevices.

**Golden-eyed Dwarf Cichlid** *Nannacara anomala* 70 mm 2¾ in. Guyana. The brown body has a greenish sheen under reflected light. The dorsal fin is long-based and edged with red and white. There is some dark patterning on the head and gill covers, and dark, vertical bars may appear on the flanks if the fish is excited or frightened. The slightly smaller female normally has dark, horizontal stripes, but extra transverse bars may appear, depending on the fish's mood, or during breeding. The eyes are golden red. A similar species, *N. taenia,* is more heavily marked with a dark, lattice-work patterning. *Temperature:* 24°C (75°F). *Diet:* live and dried foods; relishes worms of suitable size. *Breeding:* uses flowerpots, or may excavate its own preferred site. The female guards the eggs and fry and may attack the male, which should be removed after spawning.

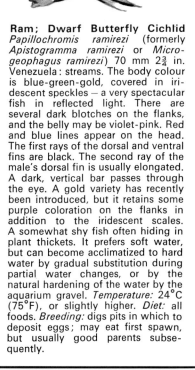

Ram

**Ram; Dwarf Butterfly Cichlid** *Papillochromis ramirezi* (formerly *Apistogramma ramirezi* or *Microgeophagus ramirezi*) 70 mm 2¾ in. Venezuela: streams. The body colour is blue-green-gold, covered in iridescent speckles – a very spectacular fish in reflected light. There are several dark blotches on the flanks, and the belly may be violet-pink. Red and blue lines appear on the head. The first rays of the dorsal and ventral fins are black. The second ray of the male's dorsal fin is usually elongated. A dark, vertical bar passes through the eye. A gold variety has recently been introduced, but it retains some purple coloration on the flanks in addition to the iridescent scales. A somewhat shy fish often hiding in plant thickets. It prefers soft water, but can become acclimatized to hard water by gradual substitution during partial water changes, or by the natural hardening of the water by the aquarium gravel. *Temperature:* 24°C (75°F), or slightly higher. *Diet:* all foods. *Breeding:* digs pits in which to deposit eggs; may eat first spawn, but usually good parents subsequently.

# ASSORTED FRESHWATER FISHES

Many smaller groups of tropical fishes contain interesting species that may be kept in the aquarium. Species of the Nandidae family are native to South America, Africa, India, Burma, Thailand and Indonesia. Most are aggressive and predatory, but their colours and behaviour ensure their popularity. Rainbowfishes and Silversides are related to the ocean Mullets. They possess two separate dorsal fins. The miscellaneous species shown here are not so widely kept as the others in this book but may be encountered occasionally. Several have unusual body shapes or swimming characteristics.

## FAMILY NANDIDAE

Nandidae

Badis

South
American
Leaf Fish

**Badis; Dwarf Chameleon Fish** *Badis badis* 65 mm  2½ in. India: standing waters. This fish can change its body colours and patterning to suit its surroundings. Generally it is a dark reddish-brown, with a greenish sheen. From time to time transverse bars may appear. The dorsal fin (similar in shape to that of Dwarf Cichlids) and caudal fin are greenish.

The female fish is less colourful. This species is not so aggressive as the rest of the family; it may be kept in the community tank, which should be heavily planted and have many hiding places. *Temperature:* 24°C (75°F). *Diet:* all foods, particularly meat and small worms. *Breeding:* spawns in caves and flowerpots, like the Dwarf Cichlids.

**South American Leaf Fish** *Polycentrus schomburgki* 90 mm  3½ in. North-eastern South America: standing waters. A stealthy, predatory fish that can swallow fishes of nearly its own length with its protrudable mouth. Its oval, pointed body (resembling a dead leaf) is light brown with dark dots. The fins are clear. At breeding time, the male turns almost black, with a cream line running from the snout to the caudal fin along the top edge of the body. *Temperature:* 24°C (75°F). *Diet:* all foods, in copious amounts. *Breeding:* eggs laid on the ceiling of caves or in flowerpots. Male fish guards the eggs; the female is best removed after spawning.

## RAINBOWFISHES AND SILVERSIDES/ FAMILY ATHERINIDAE

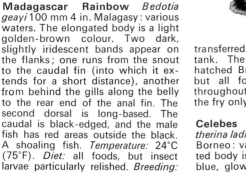

Madagascar Rainbow

Celebes Rainbow Fish

**Madagascar Rainbow** *Bedotia geayi* 100 mm 4 in. Malagasy: various waters. The elongated body is a light golden-brown colour. Two dark, slightly iridescent bands appear on the flanks; one runs from the snout to the caudal fin (into which it extends for a short distance), another from behind the gills along the belly to the rear end of the anal fin. The second dorsal is long-based. The caudal is black-edged, and the male fish has red areas outside the black. A shoaling fish. *Temperature:* 24°C (75°F). *Diet:* all foods, but insect larvae particularly relished. *Breeding:* eggs are laid over a period of days in nylon mops, from which they may be

transferred to a separate hatching tank. The fry will accept newly hatched Brine Shrimps immediately, but all foods must be circulated throughout the tank by aeration as the fry only feed at the surface.

**Celebes Rainbow Fish** *Telmatherina ladigesi* 70 mm 2¾ in. Celebes, Borneo: various waters. The elongated body is light yellow, and a light-blue, glowing line runs horizontally along the rear half. The second dorsal and the anal fin are large, with black

first rays. The male fish has filamentous extensions to these fins which give the fish a rather tattered look. The caudal fin is almost lyre-shaped, with white edging. This fish prefers hard water. *Temperature:* 24°C (75°F). *Diet:* all foods. *Breeding:* spawning mops may be used. The fry need very fine first food.

# MISCELLANEOUS SPECIES

**Long-nosed Elephant Fish** *Gnathonemus petersi* 250 mm 10 in. Africa, Cameroon: dark, turbid waters. Fishes in the Mormyridae family often have the lower lip extended into a finger-like digging tool. They also have electricity-generating cells that radiate a magnetic field around the fish, which assists navigation in the darkness. Nocturnal. *Temperature:* 24°C (75°F). *Diet:* worms and insect larvae, which should be provided in sufficient quantities to distend the stomach. *Breeding:* not yet bred in the aquarium.

**Snakehead** *Ophicephalus obscurus* 300 mm 12 in. Africa: widely distributed. This predatory fish from the Ophicephalidae family is also an excellent jumper, and its tank should be securely covered. *Temperature:* 24°C (75°F). *Diet:* worms, meat foods and young fishes. *Breeding:* the eggs float and the male guards them.

**Fire Eel** *Mastacembelus erythrotaenia* 66 mm 27 in. Thailand: various waters. A large, exotic example from the Spiny Eel family (Mastacembelidae). Other, smaller species of the genus are often finely marked and spend most of the time buried in the gravel with only the head protruding. *Temperature:* 24°C (75°F). *Diet:* worms and meat-based foods. *Breeding:* some species of *Mastacembelus* have bred in the aquarium, but no details available.

**Knife Fish; Featherback** *Notopterus chitala* 710 mm 28½ in. Burma, Malaya, Thailand: various waters. This seemingly finless fish swims with a continuous, undulating movement of the long anal fin, which fringes almost the whole length of the body. Like *Gnathonemus petersi*, it is nocturnal and navigates in the darkness in a similar fashion. *Temperature:* 24°C (75°F). *Diet:* live foods preferred, but can be weaned on to dried foods. *Breeding:* eggs are deposited on rocks, and guarded by the male.

water surface

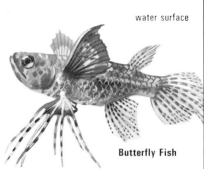

**Butterfly Fish**

**Butterfly Fish** *Pantodon bucholzi* 110 mm 4 in. West Africa: still waters. The only species in the Family Pantodontidae, *P. bucholzi* is a surface-dwelling fish with well-developed pectoral fins resembling outspread butterfly wings when viewed from above. A great jumper. *Temperature:* 25-30°C (76-86°F). *Diet:* live foods, such as crickets and beetles. *Breeding:* the fertilized eggs float, and the fry need tiny insects as first food.

**Ornate Bichir** *Polypterus ornatipinnis* 450 mm 16 in. Africa (Zaire region): rivers. The Family Polypteridae contains primitive fishes which can survive out of water. The dorsal fin is made up of a number of tiny finlets, and the fish often rests propped up on its pectoral fins. Mainly nocturnal and peaceful. *Temperature:* 24°C (75°F). *Diet:* worms, maggots and other live foods. *Breeding:* little known, but the fry have external gills at first.

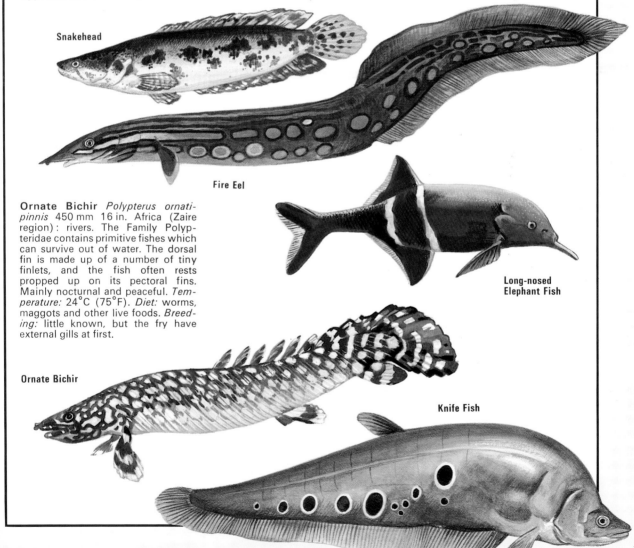

Snakehead

Fire Eel

Long-nosed Elephant Fish

Ornate Bichir

Knife Fish

# ANEMONEFISHES AND DAMSELFISHES

Most of the brilliantly coloured, tropical marine fishes are native to the coral reefs of the Indo-Pacific oceans, and to some extent to the Red Sea. Because it would be impracticable to give exact natural locations, maps showing the distribution of genera have been omitted. Unless stated otherwise, all species of marine fishes described in the following pages are kept within the temperature range 24–26°C (75–79°F) and fed with a varied diet of live foods, fresh meat and seafoods (shellfish), or suitably formulated flake foods.

In their natural habitat the Clownfishes share a fascinating relationship with the Sea-anemone (*Stoichactis*, *Discosoma* and *Radianthus* species). Normally any fish venturing into the outspread tentacles of the Sea-anemone is fatally stung and consumed, but the Clownfish enjoys immunity (and safety from other larger fishes) as it swims in and out of its host. It is assumed that in return for this favour, the Sea-anemone receives scraps of food dropped by the tenant Clownfish. Clownfishes should therefore be kept with Sea-anemones in the aquarium.

Although related to the Clownfishes, fishes of the Pomacentridea family have larger scales, and whereas the Clownfishes seek the relative safety of the Sea-anemone, the Damselfishes and Sergeant-Majors prefer to seek protection among the many coral branches of the reefs where they live. Some species have spawned in the aquarium.

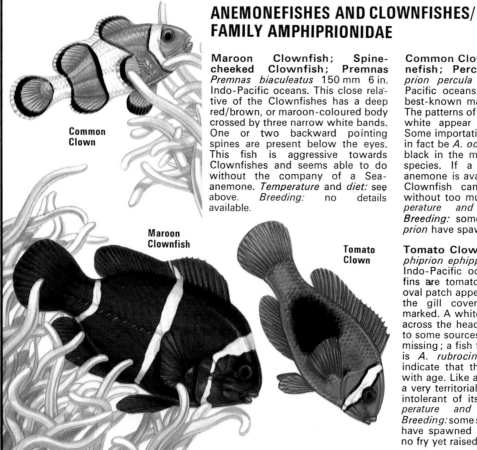

## ANEMONEFISHES AND CLOWNFISHES/ FAMILY AMPHIPRIONIDAE

**Maroon Clownfish; Spine-cheeked Clownfish; Premnas** *Premnas biaculeatus* 150 mm 6 in. Indo-Pacific oceans. This close relative of the Clownfishes has a deep red/brown, or maroon-coloured body crossed by three narrow white bands. One or two backward pointing spines are present below the eyes. This fish is aggressive towards Clownfishes and seems able to do without the company of a Sea-anemone. *Temperature* and *diet:* see above. *Breeding:* no details available.

**Common Clown**

**Maroon Clownfish**

**Tomato Clown**

**Common Clown; Clown Anemonefish; Percula Clown** *Amphiprion percula* 80 mm 3¼ in. Indo-Pacific oceans. Perhaps one of the best-known marine aquarium fishes. The patterns of red/orange, black and white appear to be hand-painted. Some importations of *A. percula* may in fact be *A. ocellaris,* which has less black in the markings than the true species. If a large enough Sea-anemone is available, more than one Clownfish can take up residence without too much squabbling. *Temperature and diet:* see above. *Breeding:* some species of *Amphiprion* have spawned in the aquarium.

**Tomato Clown; Fire Clown** *Amphiprion ephippium* 120 mm 4¾ in. Indo-Pacific oceans. The body and fins are tomato red. A blurred dark oval patch appears on the flanks, and the gill covers may be similarly marked. A white stripe runs vertically across the head, although according to some sources this stripe should be missing; a fish fitting this description is *A. rubrocinctus.* Other sources indicate that the white stripe fades with age. Like all Clownfishes, this is a very territorially minded fish and is intolerant of its own species. *Temperature and diet:* see above. *Breeding:* some species of *Amphiprion* have spawned in the aquarium, but no fry yet raised.

# DAMSELFISHES AND SERGEANT-MAJORS/ FAMILY POMACENTRIDAE

**Domino Damsel; Three Spot Damsel** *Dascyllus trimaculatus* 120 mm 4¾ in. Indo-Pacific oceans, Red Sea. An all-black fish, except for a white blotch on each flank and on the forehead. The intense black colour may fade with age. Hardy, but aggressive. *Temperature and diet:* see page 32. *Breeding:* only occasionally spawned in the aquarium.

**Humbug Damsel**

**Domino Damsel**

**Sergeant-Major**

**Yellow-tailed Blue Damsel; Saffron Blue Damsel** *Abudefduf parasema* (formerly *Pomacentrus melanochir*) 100 mm 4 in. Indo-Pacific oceans. The blue body and yellow tail become less contrasting with age as the colours lose their original intensity. There are several similarly coloured fishes in the Pomacentridae group. This species may dig in the gravel, and the under-gravel filter should be protected by a mesh in the gravel. This is a hardy species, and not so aggressive as other Damselfishes. *Temperature and diet:* see page 32. *Breeding:* no information available.

**Humbug Damsel; Black and White Damsel; White-tailed Damsel or Humbug** *Dascyllus aruanus* 80 mm 4¼ in. Indo-Pacific oceans, Red Sea. The body is silver-white and crossed by black bands, two of which slant backwards, the third being vertical. The dorsal and anal fins are black with white rear edges; the ventral fins are black; the caudal fin is white; the pectoral fins are clear. A shoaling fish which often 'adopts' a particular piece of coral or rock. Hardy, but aggressive towards other species. *Temperature and diet:* see page 32. *Breeding:* has spawned in the aquarium, but the fry not raised.

**Blue Puller** *Chromis coeruleus* 130 mm 5 in. Indo-Pacific oceans, Red Sea. A uniformly coloured blue-green fish. The dorsal fin has hard and soft rays, and the caudal fin is deeply forked. A shoaling fish which should not be kept in isolation. This fish is rather susceptible to skin infections. *Temperature and diet:* see page 32. *Breeding:* has been spawned in the aquarium.

**Yellow-backed Damsel; Black-footed Sergeant-Major; Bow-tie Damsel; Blue Fin Damsel** *Abudefduf melanopus* 70 mm 2¾ in. Indo-Pacific oceans. Also known as *Paraglyphidodon melanopus.* The bright yellow of the back and dorsal fin contrasts sharply with the grey/turquoise of the body and the black-edged turquoise ventral and anal fins. The caudal fin has yellow top and bottom edges. The eyes are yellow and turquoise, having half the eye in each coloured area of the body. Not too aggressive, but may be less hardy than other Damselfishes. *Temperature and diet:* see page 32. *Breeding:* no information available.

**Sergeant-Major** *Abudefduf saxatilis* 180 mm 7 in. Indo-Pacific oceans. The silvery-blue body has a hint of yellow on the dorsal surface, and is crossed by six dark, vertical bands. A hardy fish, but may prove too aggressive when adult. Often a leader in the dash for food, and can be relied upon to teach shy fishes, which soon learn to follow its example. *Temperature and diet:* see page 32. *Breeding:* no information available.

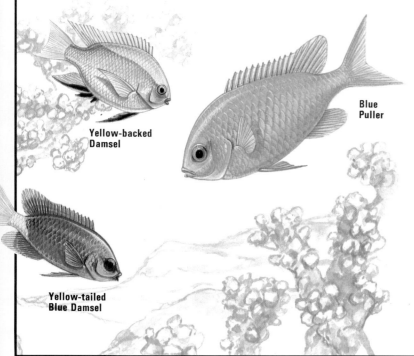

**Yellow-backed Damsel**

**Blue Puller**

**Yellow-tailed Blue Damsel**

# BUTTERFLYFISHES AND ANGELFISHES

Members of this family are deep-bodied and laterally compressed fishes. They are found mainly in the Indo-Pacific oceans, but one or two species occur in the Atlantic. They inhabit coral reefs, constantly pecking or scraping food from the surface and crevices of the coral heads. Their brilliant colours and startling patterns may be either a type of camouflage in the brightly lit world of the coral reef, or an aid in recognizing or communicating with fishes of the same species. The Angelfishes are distinguished from the Butterflyfishes by a spine at the bottom rear corner of the gill cover; many young Angelfishes have colours and markings that differ from those of the adult form. Angelfishes are territorial, and fishes of the same species will fight. Because the Butterflyfishes can be delicate, they are probably not a good choice for the novice fishkeeper. However, the bright colours are very attractive.

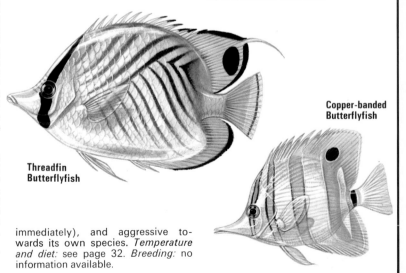

Imperial Angelfish

## BUTTERFLYFISHES AND ANGELFISHES/ FAMILY CHAETODONTIDAE

**Pakistani Butterfly; Collared Coralfish** *Chaetodon collare* 150 mm 6 in. Indo-Pacific oceans. The vulnerable eye is well-disguised in this species. A dark lattice-work pattern covers most of the body. This species is considered to be more difficult to keep than other Butterflyfishes. *Temperature and diet:* see page 32. *Breeding:* no information available.

**Threadfin Butterflyfish** *Chaetodon (Anisochaetodon) auriga* 200 mm 8 in, or slightly larger. Indo-Pacific oceans, Red Sea. Although the Butterflyfishes have a wide range of colour patterns, not many have a filamentous extension to the dorsal fin, which in this species also carries an 'eye-spot'. The function of the 'eye-spot' is to distract the attention of a predator from the real eye; for the same reason, the eyes of many species are hidden by a dark stripe. This fish is peaceful, but all Butterflyfishes appreciate a place to retreat to at night. They are shy feeders and may choose to starve rather than compete for food against more boisterous fishes in the tank. *perature and diet:* see page 32. *Breeding:* no information available.

**Copper-banded Butterflyfish; Beaked Coralfish; Long-nosed Butterflyfish** *Chelmon rostratus* 170 mm 7 in. Indo-Pacific oceans, Red Sea. The extended 'nose' of this fish is actually its mouth, and is ideally suited to picking out food from deep crevices in the coral reef. A temperamental feeder, often in reaction to changes in the water chemistry (which should be checked

**Pakistani Butterfly**

**Threadfin Butterflyfish**

**Imperial** or **Emperor Angelfish** *Pomacanthus imperator* 400 mm 16 in. Indo-Pacific oceans, Red Sea. The juvenile fish is blue with a concentric pattern of white lines, and is very similar to the juvenile forms of *P. annularis* and *P. semicirculatus.* This fish requires a clean aquarium, and the water should be partially changed regularly. *Temperature and diet:* see page 32. However, vegetable matter should be given. *Breeding:* no information available.

**Copper-banded Butterflyfish**

immediately), and aggressive towards its own species. *Temperature and diet:* see page 32. *Breeding:* no information available.

34

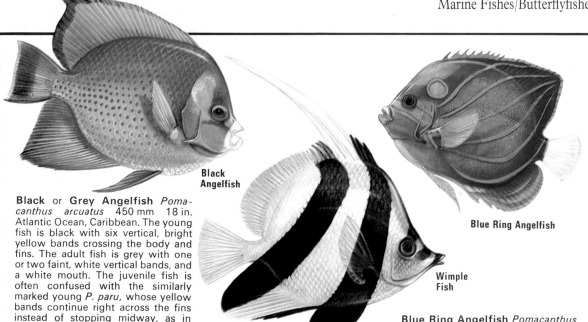

Black
Angelfish

Blue Ring Angelfish

Wimple
Fish

**Black** or **Grey Angelfish** *Poma-canthus arcuatus* 450 mm 18 in. Atlantic Ocean, Caribbean. The young fish is black with six vertical, bright yellow bands crossing the body and fins. The adult fish is grey with one or two faint, white vertical bands, and a white mouth. The juvenile fish is often confused with the similarly marked young *P. paru*, whose yellow bands continue right across the fins instead of stopping midway, as in *P. arcuatus*. *Temperature and diet:* see page 32. However, some vegetable matter should be given. *Breeding:* no information available.

**Rock Beauty** *Holacanthus tricolor* 610 mm 24½ in. Caribbean. The young fish is yellow with a blue-edged dark spot on each flank. With adulthood the spot broadens into a large dark patch. The eyes have bright blue segments. The anal and dorsal fins are edged with red. The fish's size demands that it be given a large tank, and it may bully other fishes if kept in too small an aquarium. *Temperature and diet:* see page 32. However, the diet should also include vegetable matter such as algae, spinach or lettuce. *Breeding:* no information available.

**Long-snouted Coralfish; Forceps Fish** *Forcipiger longirostris* 180 mm 7½ in, or slightly larger. Indo-Pacific oceans, Red Sea. The body shape is almost identical to that of *Chelmon rostratus*, but the coloration is entirely different. However, this fish does share the same characteristic of being a fussy feeder (although it is not so aggressive) and is not a fish for the newcomer to marine fish-keeping. *Temperature and diet:* see page 32. *Breeding:* no information available.

**Wimple Fish; Pennant Coralfish; Poor Man's Moorish Idol; Featherfin Bullfish** *Heniochus acumineatus* 200 mm 8 in. Indo-Pacific oceans, Red Sea. The sloping black stripes on the white body give the fish a leaning forward appearance, but the main physical feature is the long, banner-like dorsal fin. Easy to keep, becoming quite tame. Young specimens often act like Cleaner-fishes (see *Labroides dimidiatus*, page 37. *Temperature and diet:* see page 32. *Breeding:* no information available.

**Blue Ring Angelfish** *Pomacanthus annularis* 400 mm 16 in. Indo-Pacific oceans. The blue ring on the forward part of the brown, blue-lined body is the identifying mark of this species. The juvenile fish has many vertical, light-coloured bands and a yellow, transverse bands across the gills. The blue facial markings fade with age, and the only common characteristic between young and adult fishes is the yellow/orange caudal fin. *Temperature and diet:* see page 32. However, vegetable matter is also required. *Breeding:* no information available.

**Yellow-faced Angelfish; Blue-faced Angelfish** *Euxiphipops xanthometapon* 460 mm 18½ in. Indo-Pacific oceans. Another fish that may take a little time to settle down to aquarium life and may be a fussy feeder. Providing all the conditions, such as water composition and temperature, are satisfactory and the feeding hurdle has been overcome, the fish usually does well in the aquarium. *Temperature and diet:* see page 32. However, the diet should also include some vegetable matter. *Breeding:* no information available.

Long-snouted
Coralfish

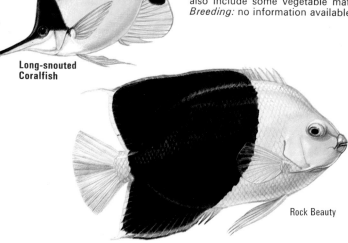

Yellow-faced
Angelfish

Rock Beauty

# SURGEONS, TRIGGERFISHES, WRASSES AND BOXFISHES

Surgeons, Tangs and Unicornfishes are brightly coloured, oval-bodied fishes with sharp, bony scalpels on the caudal peduncle which can cause painful wounds. Some species have fixed scalpels, others a protruding horn above the eyes. Triggerfishes also have a natural weapon – a spiny dorsal fin which is erected when danger threatens. Wrasses are found in all tropical seas. They often lie on the aquarium floor to rest at night, or bury themselves in the sand; others spin a mucous sleeping bag which is discarded each morning. Boxfishes and Cowfishes have bony plates covering the body instead of scales.

## SURGEONS, TANGS AND UNICORNFISHES/ FAMILY ACANTHURIDAE

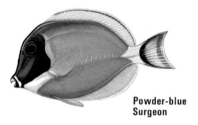

**Powder-blue Surgeon**

**Smooth-headed Unicorn Fish; Japanese Tang** *Naso lituratus* 500 mm 20 in. Indo-Pacific oceans. This fish's colour pattern gives its face a definite expression. The two fixed spines on each side of the caudal peduncle are set in bright orange patches. The outside rays of the caudal fin are pronounced. *Temperature and diet:* see page 32. However, vegetable foods should also be given. *Breeding:* no information available.

**Powder-blue Surgeon** *Acanthurus leucosternon* 300 mm 12 in. Indo-Pacific oceans. The delicate blue of the body contrasts with the black face and yellow dorsal fin. The retracted scalpel on each side of the yellow caudal peduncle can be clearly seen. A fish for the experienced marine fishkeeper, requiring plenty of swimming space and a vigorously aerated aquarium. *Temperature and diet:* see page 32. However, some vegetable food should also be provided. *Breeding:* no information available.

**Sailfin Tang** *Zebrasoma veliferum* 400 mm 16 in. Indo-Pacific oceans. The large, rounded dorsal and anal fins give an outline similar to that of the freshwater Discus (*Symphysodon*), and the body markings are also similar. The body shape is not disc-like but has the pointed, oval form normal to the Surgeonfish family. It is a hardy fish and may well become tame, accepting food from the hand. *Temperature and diet:* see page 32. However, vegetable foods should occasionally be included. *Breeding:* no information available.

**Sailfin Tang**

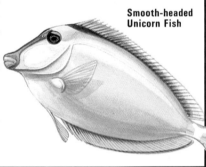

**Smooth-headed Unicorn Fish**

## TRIGGERFISHES/ FAMILY BALISTIDAE

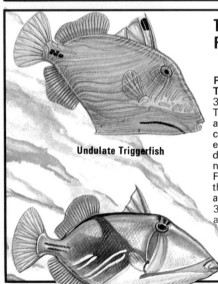

**Undulate Triggerfish**

**Picasso Trigger**

**Picasso Trigger; White-barred Triggerfish** *Rhinecanthus aculeatus* 300 mm 12 in. Indo-Pacific oceans. The abstract-art markings of this fish are the obvious inspiration for its common name, and perhaps the exaggerated mouth markings help to deter predators. The sharp teeth necessitate caution when handling. Feeding is no particular problem, but the fish may be aggressive when adult. *Temperature and diet:* see page 32. *Breeding:* no information available.

**Undulate Triggerfish; Orange-green Triggerfish** *Balistapus undulatus* 350 mm 14 in. Indo-Pacific oceans. This fish exhibits another peculiar family characteristic – that of resting head-down or lying on its side, much to the alarm of its owner. Triggerfishes have strong jaws and teeth, making the keeping of invertebrates in the same tank impracticable; they should be fed whole shellfish and small crabs to help keep their teeth worn down. Not a fussy feeder, but aggressive. *Temperature and diet:* see page 32. *Breeding:* the fish may burrow into the sand and deposit eggs in the depression; the eggs are guarded.

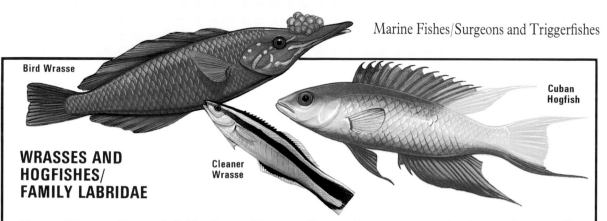

**Bird Wrasse**

**Cleaner Wrasse**

**Cuban Hogfish**

# WRASSES AND HOGFISHES/ FAMILY LABRIDAE

**Cleaner Wrasse; Cleaner Labrid** *Labroides dimidiatus* 100 mm 4 in. Indo-Pacific oceans. This fish has both female and male organs and if a dominant male in a group dies, a female fish will develop into a male to take its place. This cleaning fish has its imitators, the most notable being *Aspidontus tractus* (page 39). (These other imitators make use of their mimicry talents to approach other fishes for quite a different purpose, often leaving with a piece of flesh torn from the unsuspecting victim). *L. dimidiatus* may be clearly recognized by its terminal mouth, whereas the mouth of *A. tractus* is underslung. *Temperature and diet:* see page 32. Despite its constant attention to other fishes, this fish cannot sustain itself totally on parasites picked from the skin of other fishes, and its diet must be supplemented with finely chopped meaty foods and crumbled flake foods. *Breeding:* no information available.

**Green Wrasse; Moon Wrasse** *Thalassoma lunare* 300 mm 12 in. Indo-Pacific oceans. A beautiful fish that is constantly on the move (seemingly effortlessly so), being propelled only by the pectoral fins. A hardy fish and not a fussy feeder. It often buries itself in the sand at night. The caudal fin is crescent-shaped and the markings on the pectoral fins distinguish this fish from the very similar, but smaller, *T. lutescens.* A fairly peaceful fish, but it may worry smaller fishes. *Temperature and diet:* see page 32. *Breeding:* no information available.

**Bird Wrasse** *Gomphosus coeruleus* 270 mm 11 in. Indo-Pacific coastal waters. The adult male is cobalt blue or green with green fins, but females and young males are brownish with brown or reddish spotted scales, and

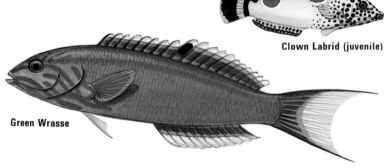

**Clown Labrid (juvenile)**

**Green Wrasse**

some red colour on the snout. The elongated snout is an excellent tool for picking out food from crevices in rocks and coral. The names *G. varius* and *G. tricolor* are sometimes seen, but may have been wrongly conferred on young specimens of *G. coeruleus. Temperature and diet:* see page 32. Also requires algae. *Breeding:* no information available.

**Cuban Hogfish** *Bodianus pulchellus* 230 mm 9 in. Caribbean. This fish is not difficult to feed, accepting shellfish meat, algae and, after a little training, flake food. Swimming is effected by the pectoral fins only, the caudal fin being used for steering only. Although the mouth is small, this fish will eagerly snap up other small fishes. *Temperature and diet:* see page 32. *Breeding:* some species of the Labridae group have spawned, but the fry have not survived.

**Clown Labrid; Twinspot Wrasse** *Coris angulata* 1220 mm 48 in. Indo-Pacific oceans. Unfortunately, the young fish soon matures and loses its colour patterns when about 100 mm long. The adult fish is green, and has yellow and purple edges to the dorsal and anal fins. Because it grows quickly, this fish is not suitable for the aquarium for very long. Other smaller species such as *C. gaimardi gaimardi, C. gaimardi africana* and *C. formosa* do not grow so fast, and the juvenile forms are also brightly coloured. *Temperature and diet:* see page 32. *Breeding:* no information available.

# BOXFISH AND COWFISH FAMILY OSTRACIIDAE

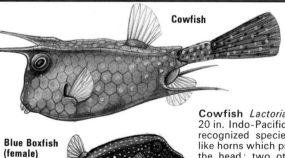

**Cowfish**

**Blue Boxfish** *Ostracion lentiginosum* 200 mm 8 in. Indo-Pacific oceans. The female fish is as illustrated but the male fish may also have a red coloration. When frightened, Boxfishes often fold their caudal fin forward along the side of the body. They may be susceptible to skin infections. *Temperature and diet:* see page 32. Brine Shrimp is often used to accustom Boxfishes to aquarium foods. *Breeding:* no information available.

**Blue Boxfish (female)**

**Cowfish** *Lactoria cornuta* 500 mm 20 in. Indo-Pacific oceans. An easily recognized species with two cow-like horns which project forward from the head · two other spines extend from the rear part of the body. *Temperature and diet:* see page 32, but small live foods preferred. *Breeding:* lays floating eggs.

# MISCELLANEOUS MARINE SPECIES

The Indo-Pacific, Pacific and Caribbean oceans are the home of an extraordinary variety of fishes, but only a small proportion of these are suitable for keeping in the home aquarium. Moreover, some of the species are incompatible with other fishes and must always be kept in separate tanks.

Several species have specialized defence mechanisms; the Beaked Leatherjacket, for example, has an erectile spine similar to those of the Triggerfishes (page 36) while Batfishes may secrete poisonous mucus when in danger. More aggressive is the Lionfish which kills its victims with its poisonous spines. It is difficult to keep as it requires live food, often eating six or so fishes a day. Another species which needs live food is the Spotted Sea-horse.

**Royal Gramma; Fairy Basslet** *Gramma loreto* 80 mm 3 in. Caribbean. A startlingly coloured fish which spends most of its time in caves and other hiding places. It is a member of the Basslet family (Grammidae), which are similar to, but less aggressive than, the Serranidae group. Because this fish is a good jumper the aquarium should be covered at all times. A similar species is the False Gramma, or Royal Dottyback (*Pseudochromis paccagnella*), whose identical colours are separated by a narrow white band. *Temperature and diet:* see page 32. *Breeding:* the male builds a nest of algae and small pieces of coral. Eggs have been observed in the aquarium, but no fry have been raised.

**Neon Goby** *Elactinus oceanops* 60 mm 2½ in. Caribbean, Like their freshwater relations, the saltwater Gobies (Family Gobiidae) spend most of their time scurrying around the aquarium floor. The Neon Goby is similar in body shape and markings to the Cleaner Wrasse (*Labroides dimidiatus*, page 37), and it performs a limited cleaning service for other fishes in the aquarium. *Temperature and diet:* see page 32. *Breeding:* has been spawned in the aquarium. Adults guard the eggs and young.

**Mandarin Fish**

**Royal Gramma**

**Mandarin Fish** *Synchiropus splendidus* 70 mm 3 in. Indo-Pacific oceans. Mandarin Fishes and Dragonets (Family Callionymidae) inhabit tidal rock pools. This species, like many other males of the family, has an elongated first dorsal fin. Its common name derives from the oriental-looking colour patterns on the body. It seems to do best if kept on its own, but is difficult to acclimatize to aquarium foods. *Temperature and diet:* see page 32. *Breeding:* no information available.

**Beaked Leatherjacket** *Oxymonocanthus longirostris* 80 mm 3 in. Indo-Pacific oceans. A headstanding fish of bizarre coloration belonging to the Filefish and Leatherjacket family (Monocanthidae). These have an erectile spine that can be locked into place. No ventral fins are present, but a membrane is stretched across the projecting pelvic bones. This fish will eat any live corals, Crustaceans and Tubeworms occupying the same aquarium, and should be kept in small groups in a quiet tank, as it will pine away if alone. *Temperature and diet:* see page 32, but diet should include vegetable matter. Somewhat difficult to accustom to aquarium foods. *Breeding:* no information available.

**Beaked Leatherjacket**

**Round Batfish**

**Neon Goby**

**Round Batfish** *Platax orbicularis* 500 mm 20 in. Indo-Pacific oceans. Members of the Batfish family (Platacidae) are characterized by their disc-shaped bodies, while the juvenile forms also have extremely elongated fins. It is believed that Batfishes can release a poisonous mucus into the water as a defence mechanism. Some confusion surrounds the exact number of species; some sources treat *P. orbicularis* and *P. teira* as synonyms for *P. pinnatus*, whereas others regard all three as separate species. Batfishes appreciate a tall, spacious tank, and young specimens soon outgrow the aquarium. Although they are peaceful and can become tame, they are easily frightened. *Temperature and diet:* see page 32. *Breeding:* no information available.

**Spotted Sea-horse; Golden Sea-horse** *Hippocampus kuda* 300 mm 12 in, smaller in the aquarium. Indo-Pacific oceans. This fish, which everyone knows and wants to keep in the aquarium, belongs to the Sea-horse and Pipefish family (Syngnathidae). It swims in a vertical or forward-slanting position, and anchors itself to branches of coral or a Sea Fan. Other species of Sea-horses include *H. hudsonius* and *H. zosterae,* both Atlantic Ocean species. *Temperature and diet:* see page 32. However, small live foods are essential, even young freshwater Guppy fry. *Breeding:* the male fish incubates fertilized eggs in its abdominal pouch.

**Red Squirrelfish** *Holocentrus ruber* 230 mm 9 in. Indo-Pacific oceans, Red Sea. The Holocentridae family, comprising Squirrelfishes and Soldierfishes, are predatory, nocturnal fishes which hide in crevices during the daytime. In this species, the usual red coloration of the family is broken by lighter-coloured horizontal bands. The large eyes indicate the fish's nocturnal nature. *Temperature and diet:* see page 32. *Breeding:* some species of Holocentridae have been seen to spawn in the aquarium.

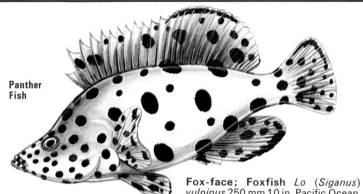

Panther Fish

**Panther Fish; Polka Dot Grouper; Barramundi Cod** *Cromileptes altivelis* 500 mm 20 in. Indo-Pacific oceans. A beautiful representative of the Serranidae family, comprising Rock Cods and Groupers, which are large predatory fishes without ventral fins. The white body and fins of this species are speckled with large black dots. It is a very hardy fish, but should only be kept with fishes of its own size. *Temperature and diet:* see page 32. *Breeding:* no information available.

**Fox-face; Foxfish** *Lo* (*Siganus*) *vulpinus* 250 mm 10 in. Pacific Ocean. A member of the Spinefeet and Rabbitfish family (Siganidae), which are similar in shape to the Surgeonfishes (Family Acanthuridae, see page 36), but have no scalpels on the caudal peduncle. They normally swim head-downwards, and most of the family are herbivorous. This species is the exception in the family in possessing a tubular snout with a terminal mouth. The spines of its dorsal fin are poisonous. *Temperature and diet:* see page 32. However, vegetable matter should also be provided. *Breeding:* no information available.

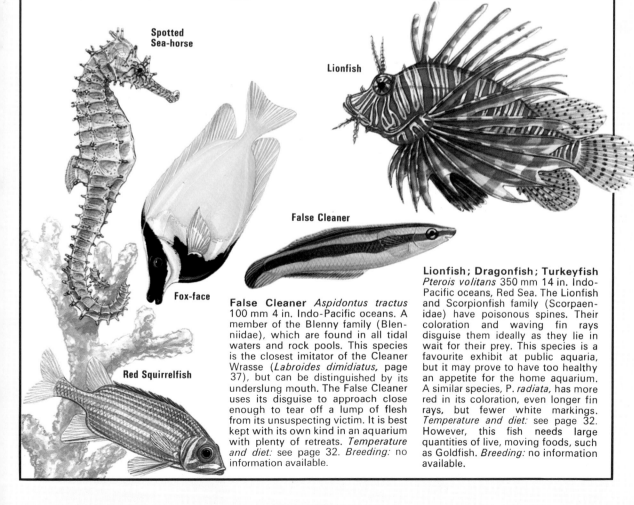

Spotted Sea-horse

Lionfish

False Cleaner

Fox-face

Red Squirrelfish

**False Cleaner** *Aspidontus tractus* 100 mm 4 in. Indo-Pacific oceans. A member of the Blenny family (Blenniidae), which are found in all tidal waters and rock pools. This species is the closest imitator of the Cleaner Wrasse (*Labroides dimidiatus,* page 37), but can be distinguished by its underslung mouth. The False Cleaner uses its disguise to approach close enough to tear off a lump of flesh from its unsuspecting victim. It is best kept with its own kind in an aquarium with plenty of retreats. *Temperature and diet:* see page 32. *Breeding:* no information available.

**Lionfish; Dragonfish; Turkeyfish** *Pterois volitans* 350 mm 14 in. Indo-Pacific oceans, Red Sea. The Lionfish and Scorpionfish family (Scorpaenidae) have poisonous spines. Their coloration and waving fin rays disguise them ideally as they lie in wait for their prey. This species is a favourite exhibit at public aquaria, but it may prove to have too healthy an appetite for the home aquarium. A similar species, *P. radiata,* has more red in its coloration, even longer fin rays, but fewer white markings. *Temperature and diet:* see page 32. However, this fish needs large quantities of live, moving foods, such as Goldfish. *Breeding:* no information available.

# INDEX